new roles for YOUTH in the school and the community

945-1

National Commission on Resources for Youth

CITATION PRESS   NEW YORK   1974

Cover design by Lucy Bitzer

Contents

Acknowledgements

In a book of this kind that has accrued over a five-year period, we find ourselves indebted to many people—too many to mention each by name. The programs described were selected from hundreds of examples brought to the attention of the Commission by friends across the country who, like ourselves, are seeking to facilitate the efforts of young people to assume responsible roles in society. We are deeply grateful to the directors and staff of each of the programs described. They opened wide their doors for visitations by our staff and consultants and gave generously of their time in reading and responding to our reports.

In developing the basic viewpoints expressed in the book we had the advantage of exciting and continual discussion with members of the Board of Directors of the Commission and our consultants. We also received help from members of a group, half of whom were educators and half students, who convened for a meeting on May 23 and 24, 1970. Later some of these individuals observed and reported on programs.

We are particularly grateful to Mora and Alec Dickson of the Community Service Volunteers of London, England, who spent two months with us visiting projects on the West Coast that had been recommended to us by Ruth Chance, Director of the Rosenberg Foundation in San Francisco. We benefitted greatly from the insights offered by these three friends as to what makes a project successful.

In addition, we wish to thank the following consultants who generously gave their time to examine programs and share with us their wide experience in the education of young people: Patricia Allen, Bruce Dollar, Sr. Ruth Dowd, Don Eberle, Estelle Fuchs, Gary Griffin, Mildred McClosky, Sr. Eileen O'Gorman, Marcia Perlstein, John Rude, and William Soskin.

We are indebted to Jeff Lewis for organizing the many reports into a first draft of the book and to Dorothy Neubauer for her painstaking editing of the final product.

As Executive Director of the Commission, I want to thank the following staff, past and present, who contributed to this book, always in addition to their regular staff duties: Chitra Karunakaran, Lorraine Kavanagh, Peter Kleinbard, Norman Mathews, Phyllis Wachsman, and Louise Youngquist.

Last but not least, we wish to express our appreciation to the Ford Foundation for the grant that made this product possible, and to Ed Meade, who has been a good project officer, always encouraging and facilitating but not dominating.

MARY CONWAY KOHLER
Director

Foreword

The National Commission on Resources for Youth was established because of the increasing difficulty young people find today in making the transition from adolescence to constructive adult life. In earlier periods the home, the local community, and the place of employment furnished a variety of opportunities for youth to work, to make helpful contributions to family and community, and to associate in other ways with adults. As they grew older this enabled them to participate more and more in adult activities and to assume an increasing degree of responsibility. In this way they gained both competence and assurance that they were moving successfully into adulthood.

This situation has changed. The specialization of contemporary society, the reduction, and in many cases the elimination, of home chores, limitations placed on youth employment, greater emphasis upon youth protection rather than production, and the high degree of age stratification in urban activities have greatly isolated adolescents from the adult world and blocked the pathways through which the young move into mature roles in society.

The National Commission's purpose is to find and make widely known examples of successful programs that have overcome these blockades and enabled young people to participate in productive adult activities and to assume real responsibility for what they do. To accomplish this objective it has developed a network of people, largely volunteers, and organizations that are on the lookout for promising programs. As these are identified, the Commission seeks to obtain impartial external appraisals of their effectiveness and their potential usefulness in other communities. In some cases, programs validated in this way have become demonstration projects such as Youth Tutoring Youth and Youth Helper in Day Care; the responsibility for the demonstration is undertaken by the Commission. To disseminate information about projects, the Commission publishes *Resources for Youth*, a newsletter with a wide circulation.

Within the limits of its resources, the Commission also provides technical assistance to community groups that wish to adopt and adapt a program for their own use. This assistance includes such things as: suggestions on ways of getting the program sponsored, advice about organizing and administering it, and help in training personnel for the new activities involved.

The National Commission on Resources for Youth was created in 1967 as a kind of spontaneous action by a group of educators, social scientists, judges, and businessmen who had long been concerned with the well-being of youth. The decision to form a small organization was made as they discussed the difficulties young people face in making a constructive transition to adult life. They believed that such an organization could be of significant help in opening the channels for youth development by working with major institutions such as the schools and voluntary agencies in developing, improvising, and expanding programs in which young persons can find more opportunities to participate actively and responsibly in the world around them.

The Director of the Commission is Judge Mary Conway Kohler who works with a small staff, a larger group of part-time associates, and a much larger band of volunteers. This kind of organization is particularly effective in making firsthand contact with promising programs and providing a variety of personal observations as well as more formal descriptions and appraisals. This type of organization is necessary because the United States is a very large country, and it is not surprising that dozens of promising programs are brought to the attention of the Commission every month. Although most communities have not thus far broken the blockades that interfere with the transition of their youth into responsible adulthood, a few have, and they are to be found in all areas of the nation.

As programs are brought to the attention of the Commission, arrangements for appraising them must be worked out because, unfortunately, many projects that are initially identified as promising turn out, upon careful study, to be of doubtful value for others either because they do not provide for the wholehearted, responsible participation of youth, or because they involve features that are not feasible for wide adoption or adaptation. The projects reported in this book have been studied, and they are judged to be examples that do provide opportunities for youth to take initiative and to carry on activities that are socially constructive and productive and for which young people can take the major responsibilities. Furthermore, all of the seven types of programs described have been developed in varying forms in a number of communities, thus indicating their potential for wider use.

Some of the specific projects described are not now in existence, even though they were operating energetically and effectively when visited by the Commission staff or associates. The fact that some specific projects initiated and effectively carried out by youth have relatively short lives is to be expected and does not represent defects in them. As today's young people become adults, younger ones become adolescents. Each new group of youth will wish to initiate new projects or create others in new forms. A program that continues unchanged for some years is likely to have lost the interest of the current group and also its vitality. New ideas emerge and new energy creates new projects.

The seven types of youth programs described here are not believed to be an inclusive list of all kinds now in existence, but they do represent a variety of the kinds of personal roles and forms of expression through which young people may make significant social contributions. The Commission hopes that its descriptions will stimulate individuals and groups to develop a still larger variety of vital projects in which youth create their own constructive transition into maturity. As I have learned of these programs, I have gained greater optimism about the development of youth today. Projects of the kinds described clearly demonstrate that youth can be tremendous assets to society rather than burdens.

Recently, public attention has been called to the difficult transition of youth by a panel of the President's Science Advisory Committee, by a group appointed by the Kettering Foundation, by a Commission of the U.S. Department of Health, Education and Welfare, and by the National Association of Secondary School Principals' National Committee on Secondary Education. Several of these groups have proposed extensive reforms of society and the establishment of new institutions. The programs outlined in this book are examples of ways by which youth transition can be greatly aided within the framework of our existing social institutions. It is possible now to help young people without waiting until more profound restructuring of society takes place.

RALPH W. TYLER, Chairman
National Commission on Resources for Youth

given a chance

What I was trying to accomplish so desperately and too desperately, I think, was that rarely given, but absolutely beautiful sign of involvement on the face of each individual kid. Their faces just light up for a short time, and you could just see their minds working at some solution or some problem of thinking and feeling and imagining. Their eyes open wide, their voices become louder and their mouths smile.

We do it mainly because we want to help this community out. Most people here really are poor. But it's also something for us to do. It helps us to grow right. But mainly it helps the little kids. Because they really don't know what to do. And then they see us. And maybe one day they'll think about what we did and try to do it.

Do young Americans care about what happens to anybody but themselves and their with-it generation?

This book is evidence that a lot of them *do* care. They care about themselves, of course, and they should. They also care about other people, although sometimes it is necessary to cut through their seeming indifference and defensiveness to discover the depth of their caring.

They care enough to set up and operate projects in which they help their peers cope with adolescent problems: alienation from adults, running away from home, drug abuse, need for recreational facilities, need for appropriate peer and adult models with whom they can identify, need for development of self-esteem and a sense of personal direction, and need for gainful employment.

Many young people care enough to spend hours working with handicapped people—young and old—and to precede and accompany their work with training programs that help to make them knowledgeable and more effective as they carry on their tasks.

They care enough to serve as tutors for young children and to prepare themselves to understand their youthful charges and develop diverse ways to help them.

They care enough to become involved in many worthwhile community activities: building low income housing, publishing newspapers and magazines geared to the needs of a specific community, or working with painstaking care to help archeologists find and preserve the evidences of earlier cultures before being obliterated by the bulldozers of "progress."

Descriptions of these and many other youth involvement projects are included in *New Roles for Youth in the School and the Community*, a book prepared by the National Commission on Resources for Youth. This Commission is a nonprofit organization actively involved in identifying youth participation projects across the United States, and maintaining a file of such projects as a basis for disseminating information about them to schools and other institutions interested in pursuing similar actvities. Most of the projects are school related in some way and reflect the increasing sensitivity to the value of involving youth in a wide variety of active work experiences that can take place within the school, the church, nonprofit agencies, or out in the community. Each project is adaptable for use by one or all such organizations.

To determine ways in which young people can be constructively involved in such projects, it is essential to take a close look at today's society and at young people themselves—what they are like and the problems they face in today's world. For example, adults, particularly, must remind themselves that our once agrarian, pre-technology society, with its genuine need for large numbers of unskilled labor, has vanished. Today, gainful employment for the unskilled adult is increasingly difficult to find; for the majority of unskilled youth it is next to impossible.

The nature of family living has changed, too. The large family that once made it obviously necessary for children and youth to help look after one another and to share the tasks of daily living is disappearing. The shift away from the extended family removes both youth and adults from many cross-age contacts. Almost without our realizing it, we find ourselves living in a world in which youth speaks mainly to youth and adults speak mainly to adults.

Some important changes in the physiological development of youth are taking place, too. Young people today are moving more quickly to puberty and are reaching their physical growth level in a shorter period of time. This early and rapid maturation accentuates the problems of adolescents.

Psychologically the needs and desires of youth continue to maintain a fairly consistent pattern. Young people today, like their predecessors, want to be respected for themselves as individuals and for their achievements. They want to have a part in the decisions that affect them. They want to have friends, to love and be loved. They want to play, to create, to work, to produce. They want the satisfaction of helping others and the challenge of developing skills that make it possible for them to provide competent help.

What can be done? What can be done to find worthwhile roles for youth in the kind of society we live in today?

There are literally thousands of ways to use the resources of youth and many of them are being explored. The unmet needs in our society are so great that there should be a place for any young person who wants to make a contribution. Equally important, a young person's need to be needed cannot long be ignored without significant loss to his self-esteem and to his present and future achievement and personal satisfaction. The opportunities for young people to serve are constantly expanding as schools, government agencies, and other youth-serving groups recognize the importance of involving youth in many varieties of work projects.

New Roles for Youth in the School and the Community describes a great many projects in which young peope have been and are being productively involved in activities that have value for themselves and for other people. This book reports what many people—youth and adults—have done and are doing to: (*1*) identify the needs and concerns of youth and of society, (*2*) identify the resources young people have for dealing with these problems, and (*3*) put youth resources to constructive use in dealing with the concerns and problems that are identified.

In the next seven chapters are descriptions of many ways in which the resources of youth are extending the horizons of learning, improving the quality of learning, and providing a remarkable variety of benefits to people of all ages. There are descriptions of ways in which young people are working with one another, with teachers, school administrators, and boards of education, and with people in institutions outside the school framework in successful efforts to cope with some of the problems of young people and of the adult society as well.

The projects selected for inclusion in *New Roles for Youth in the School and the Community* are representative of some of the many opportunities for effective youth involvement. Those who have had experience with these and comparable projects strongly believe that youth participation is probably the most important single ingredient of a successful program. Youth participation includes many things: it includes freedom and support to raise questions, help identify problems, contribute ideas, plan for action, make decisions, follow through, evaluate (evaluate processes, procedures, and results), make changes, and evaluate again. Admittedly, the nature and extent of youth involvement varies with the nature of each project, with the age and maturity levels of the young people, with the attitudes and skills of the adult supervisors, and with the total setting within which a project operates.

Not all of the projects selected for inclusion in *New Roles for Youth in the School and the Community* represent the ultimate in youth participation. In fact, probably no such project can exist, but in each program described young people have been active participants with continuing opportunities for being involved in making decisions and for taking a major responsibility for planning and operating a project.

The programs reported were selected by the National Commission on Resources for Youth from literally hundreds of youth-involvement projects being carried on in various parts of the United States. Choices had to be made, and by no means could all of the worthwhile projects be included. Aside from the need to avoid the repetition that could come from describing projects that are similar in many respects, and aside from the need to hold the book to a reasonable length, there was also the desire to make the book practical and widely usable by its readers. Several questions, therefore, served as guides for determining which projects should be included. For example:

Does the project have social or educational significance for contemporary youth? Do the young people involved feel the project is important?

Do young people play important roles in the project? Have they initiated it? Have they run it or helped run it? Have their needs and their skills created the style and direction of the program?

Is the project innovative in some way? Does it either represent a new approach or an old one with a new twist for today's youth?

Does the project have growth potential for youth? Are young people gradually taking on more responsible roles within the program? Are they developing attitudes and skills that can eventually help them towards better citizenship, better work skills, and increased self-fulfillment?

Has the project lasted long enough to test the validity of its goals, its effectiveness in achieving goals, its flexibility for change as change seems needed? Are there any evaluations or progress reports available?

Most important, is the project one that could be replicated in other schools or communities in different parts of the country? Is it a project that lends itself to adaptation?

As the selected projects clearly indicate, young people can achieve a great deal on their own; they have proved it many times. But one point that is stressed repeatedly, in these and other comparable projects, is the importance of appropriate adult support. The kind of support that seems most valuable is based on an understanding of youth and of the social context in which problems arise and must be resolved; it is support that is based on genuine confidence in the dedication and the competence of youth; support that is based on a realistic appraisal, shared with youth, of the skills and the knowledge needed for effective project participation; it is support for finding ways to develop and use the necessary skills.

Each chapter in *New Roles for Youth in the School and*

the Community has a special focus as its title indicates: Youth as Curriculum Builders, Youth as Teachers, Youth as Community Manpower, Youth as Entrepreneurs, Youth as Community Problem-Solvers, Youth as Communicators, and Youth as Resources for Youth. This is an organizational device to help the reader identify areas that may be of particular interest to him. One fact that should be noted, however, particularly by those who are interested in curriculum building, is that ideas on this topic are not restricted to the chapter titled Youth as Curriculum Builders. Every chapter in the book contains suggestions—explicit or implied—for ways in which a school program may be modified by student involvement.

As you read, you will note that some of the projects described are no longer in existence. It is reasonable to anticipate, too, that in the time intervening between the collection of data and the published report, still other project changes will have taken place. But it is important to bear in mind that in youth involvement programs, change is an inevitable and a desirable element. The concerns of one group of young people are not necessarily the concerns of a succeeding group. Indeed, one of the values of youth participation projects is the acceptance of responsibility for identifying concerns and for devising means to deal with them. People involved in youth projects feel it is essential to be flexible enough to drop a project when it no longer serves a function, to make needed changes as situations vary, or to try something totally different. In some of the ongoing programs, young people who are about to leave often undertake to train younger students who will be taking over. But here again, effective student trainers are imbued with the idea of flexibility and do not seek, in their training techniques, to impose on their successors a precise system of operation.

For the young person or adult who may be interested in developing a project similar to one described, the important question is: "Does this project, or one somewhat like it but adapted to our local situation, seem to have real potential for youth?"

New Roles for Youth in the School and the Community seeks to do two things: (*1*) provide descriptions of a number of youth involvement projects that seem to have made significant contributions to young people, their schools, and their communities and (*2*) provide information that may be useful to others who wish to initiate youth involvement projects. The descriptions themselves should help provide information for starting and operating youth projects. They usually explain how a particular project began, mention the important problems encountered, indicate the kind of support needed for operating the project, and so on. To supplement this information, however, there is a final chapter, Now What?, that contains still further suggestions that may serve as useful guidelines.

YOUTH
as curriculum builders

When we opened the doors of our little laboratory at
Enfield High School three years ago, we decided that
enough people were already talking about what
couldn't be done—and that we should start doing what
could be done. Essentially education is the individual's
search for meaning in his own life. But you can't find
meaning sitting in a chair; you can't get it poured
into you; you have to get up and find it for yourself.

It seemed like I never had a say in anything. I always
felt that no one listened. Then I started working with
Students Concerned with Public Health. And I could see
what I said made a difference.

We offer the elementary school students an alternative
to the self- and community-defeating behavior of gang
warfare, drugs, and empty rhetoric by showing the
tremendous need for manpower in health. And we show
them ourselves that we are examples of how students
can "turn on" with people and bring about change,
and the pride and satisfaction that result.

For many years, regardless of whatever other privileges and opportunities were granted to students in the public schools, the job of building a curriculum for them was left almost exclusively in the hands of their teachers and outside experts in content and methodology. Of course there were modest exceptions, but generally a student had little choice as to the content of what he was supposed to study or the manner in which that content was presented to him. The assumptions underlying this rule seemed to be that (1) students have relatively few experiences that would provide educational content worth taking school time to convey to their classmates and (2) students lack the breadth and mental discipline needed to help develop learning programs.

In the last few years, however, things have been happening that to a certain extent seem to undermine these assumptions. The first of these is the impingement of the outside world on the world of the classroom. More and more it seems that events that are going on outside the school walls significantly affect the student's present and will affect his future. These issues and events should, therefore, be acknowledged as having a valid place in the school curriculum.

A second phenomenon is the increased sophistication of many students—sophistication brought about in part through the influence of the mass media.

The third phenomenon is the much discussed communications gap between many adults and many students. This gap may well suggest that some students learn more readily from materials prepared by other students than they learn from materials prepared entirely by adults.

When students have a chance to participate in the preparation of learning materials for other students, they seem to enjoy it immensely. They work with diligence, eagerness, and discipline, and they themselves derive educational benefits that are as significant as the benefits accruing to the student recipients of their endeavors. This discovery, perhaps more than any other single factor, has led many schools during the past few years to embark on programs that give students opportunities to develop curricula to be used by other students.

This chapter will examine closely two such programs and will provide a few significant details about several others. It must not be assumed, of course, that these cover either the range of programs now in existence or the range of possible programs that an imaginative school district might devise. Curriculum development is a vast field, and the talents and needs of young students are many. In the coming years schools will surely devise ever-increasing numbers of ways in which students may be both creators and users of school curricula.

It should be noted, too, that although this chapter focuses on student involvement in curriculum development, *every* chapter in this book points out ways students are contributing, either directly or indirectly, to curricular change and development.

THE SOCIAL STUDIES LABORATORY
ENFIELD, CONNECTICUT

Enfield is an old mill town located on the Connecticut River in the north-central part of the state. Its some forty-eight thousand residents are largely lower-middle and middle class and tend to be conservative in outlook. It would be easy to assume that such a community would be an unlikely setting for a bold and fresh innovation in its school program, but Enfield High School has a social studies program that is truly bold and innovative—and it was started by a junior.

This young man wanted the school to have a place where students could go to make films and tapes—useful studies, really—of topics that were of special interest to them. One night at a rehearsal for a school play, he happened to see the chairman of the social studies department. He told the chairman about his idea, and later they discussed it at some length. They felt they were onto something that might excite imaginations in the social studies area. They wrote proposals, obtained some funds and equipment, and the Enfield Social Studies Laboratory soon became a reality. The Laboratory's student-founder described his idea this way:

The purpose of the Laboratory is to show kids how to learn for themselves; to help them find themselves by getting involved, really involved, in their own education.

From the very beginning the Social Studies Laboratory was very different from any other place in Enfield High School. It was a place where some students did very serious and arduous work; it was also a place where students felt free to simply come to sit and talk. It was a place where some students worked for credit by prearrangement with a teacher and others worked equally hard or harder for no credit at all. It was a place where some of Enfield's most successful students worked side by side with some of its least successful, with great value to both groups. The students ran the Lab themselves. They considered it their own—and the place was full after school as well as during school hours.

The Lab's first director was the sixteen-year-old who conceived the idea in 1967 and who, in 1968, developed a new idea to expand the usefulness of the Lab's nucleus of cameras and tape recorders. The school's social studies chairman described the conversation about this new idea:

It was a hot June afternoon in 1968. [He] stopped me in the school corridor.

"Been working on an idea," he said. "Lots of cities, like New York, have a setup where they record their history on tape. Supposing we went them one better and set up a center where we preserve this town's heritage in both sight and sound— letting the kids do the job!"

As we walked into the Lab, he began to fill in the ideas with swift sketches on the blackboard.

"We start with relevance. We ask kids what they like about this town and what bugs them. Maybe it's being chased off the plaza by the police or the need for a pool. Look up the street. The old town hall is two hundred years old, but the roof is falling in! And we have other great landmarks, like the old Congregational Church."

Swiftly his chalk scrawled questions across the board: What does an expressway do to a community? How can we save our landmarks? What happens to a Puerto Rican if he comes here to live?

Then he continued: "So we create small teams of two or three kids and a teacher who shares a concern about something. We send them out into the field with cameras and tape recorders. They learn how to ask questions and take pictures that tell the story. Then they bring the stuff back to the Lab, put it together with a synchronized sound track, and we use the unit to teach the other kids what makes their town tick."

Then he jotted more notes on the blackboard.

"That's just the beginning. The point is, we keep the units together, slides synchronized with sound. And year by year we become more than a Social Studies Laboratory, more than a school—we also become a Living History Center for the town. The archives, the place where you keep the heritage forever!"

Once again, this student's vision became a reality. During the following days, he pounded on doors to ask for support. He gained the school superintendent's support with the argument that the Center would contribute to the improvement of school-community relations. Other school officials were impressed by his statement that this was a compact, practical kind of innovation that required no new courses or curriculum changes. He then went to Rochester, New York, to meet with officials of the Eastman Kodak Company, and he returned with pledges of cameras, film, slide projectors, and synchronizer units. The Living History Center of the Enfield High School Social Studies Laboratory was off the ground, and in the fall of 1968 Enfield students were out in the field—interviewing, photographing, taping, creating, and preserving.

Among the early sound-slide projects completed at the Center were: "Our Vanishing Heritage," a study of Enfield landmarks; "The New Breed: Class of 1969," which showed how adults as well as members of the class viewed the class's values; "Men in Blue," documenting the relationships among police, the community, and youth; and "Fermi: A School Is Born," which traced the building of a new high school from its planning stages (in which students participated) to its completion.

The Living History Center was by no means the Laboratory's only innovative activity. Its students have also created publications: *Contact*, a bimonthly journal designed to stimulate faculty-student dialogue on social science issues (now defunct); *Future*, an annual of scholarly, annotated articles written by students; and two pamphlets, *The Creative Impulse* and *How to Start a Living History Center*, describing Lab programs and giving tips on how similar programs can be started in other schools.

Another creative project that expanded the scope and usefulness of the Lab was the development of what students decided to call Lab-Carts. The physical structure of a Lab-Cart is simple: it consists of a compact set of shelves mounted on casters so that it can be moved about easily. Each Lab-Cart houses a carefully prepared set of multimedia materials on some specific topic—Africa, the military-industrial complex, Indian lore, and so on. A tape recorder and a Carousel projector are mounted on the top of the Lab-Cart for the presentation of sound-slide units. An introductory unit shows and tells how to use the Lab-Cart materials effectively, stimulates interest in the subject, and usually includes several specific slides on the topic of the Cart. Other sound-slide units may be part of the study materials. Thus, a Lab-Cart provides both materials and methods for creative learning, and these materials and methods are themselves the product of creative learning.

Although the Lab-Cart was originally designed for social studies, the idea can readily be adapted for use with many other areas of study. This has already happened at Enfield High as will be noted later in the discussion of the expanding Lab projects.

In creating a Lab-Cart, students do all the things they did when the Lab first opened its doors—gather materials, conduct research, prepare sound-slide shows—but they do them in a more thorough manner, they use more sophisticated skills, and they work in a fairly large team. Each single topic Cart is designed to support the interests of whole classes of students, and its wheels enable it to enter any classroom easily. In fact, to permit demonstration to other schools and community groups, the Carts were designed to fit into the backseat of a Volkswagen!

Each Cart is stocked with a wide variety of materials to satisfy individual tastes and abilities. In addition to the introductory sound-slide unit designed to stimulate interest in the Cart and to instruct students how to use its materials, there are books, reprints, additional sound-slide sets, bibliographies, and a list of outside sources, places to visit, and speakers. Materials on a single subject may present the diverse perspectives of geographers, historians, anthropologists, and economists. The Carts are intended to stimulate the proper use of the inquiry process. Moreover, Lab-Carts allow for continuous curriculum revision. If a current event sparks interest in a subject such as the Vietnam War, or student rebellion, or corruption in government, that subject can be readily integrated into the curriculum with materials provided for immediate use and future inquiry. When students request a course in black studies or the military-industrial complex, they can develop Lab-Carts on those subjects and try them out in the classroom. If the Carts are successful, the school can develop a course on the topic. For instance, a new course was offered during 1970–71 as the result of one student's Lab-Cart on Canada.

One of the best aspects of the Lab-Cart idea is that it is basically uncomplicated and can be adopted on a trial basis by another school district. All that is really needed to start a Cart is some wood, some casters, and the basic audio-visual equipment most schools already have. How does one actually produce a Lab-Cart? Enfield High School has recorded the basic processes for use by other schools. The following advice, drawn from a Laboratory pamphlet written for teachers, seems particularly helpful:

Starting a Lab Cart

STEP 1: PICKING A SUBJECT

Let us assume that a student has come to you, the teacher, and said that he wants to start a Lab-Cart about the American Indian.

Don't put him to work answering your questions. LET HIM ASK HIS OWN QUESTIONS.

The questions he will come up with are likely to be very generalized, very broad in scope, vaguely stated. That's all right. He will learn to focus the questions more sharply with immersion in the process.

STEP 2: HELP THE STUDENT MAKE A PRELIMINARY SEARCH FOR SOURCES

Help the student find a wide variety of exciting sources . . . television . . . first-hand interviews with "experts" (including Indians) . . . filmstrips . . . museum artifacts . . . books . . .

A student-built Lab-Cart serves as a resource library for students and teachers for mini-courses.   MATT SKYPEK, JR.

STEP 3: HELP THE STUDENT LEARN BASIC RESEARCH SKILLS

He needs to learn how to make a simple bibliography and note card, how to abstract the key ideas, and how to make a reasonably correct evaluation of the worth of the material. Help him learn to understand the need for some criteria for forming judgments: How recent is the material? How accurate? How relevant to what he wants to know?

STEP 4: MAKE AN OUTLINE OF THE AREAS OF INQUIRY

In many cases, the student will want to ask questions . . . from an inter-disciplinary point of view to determine the effects of geography, economics, history, life-style. A great strength of Lab-Cart learning is that the student discovers that there are many ways to look at things, many paths to learning.

You will probably have to help the student at this point to limit the scope of his questions . . . Often research ends up resembling the Rio Grande River—thirty miles wide and six inches deep. The Lab-Carts must have *depth* rather than broad survey coverage.

STEP 5: MAKE A LAB-CART PLAN WITH REASONABLE DEADLINES

This should be worked out jointly between teacher and student. There are dangers at both extremes. . . .

STEP 6: LET GOOD RESEARCH TAKE PLACE

We mean that it should be done willingly and enthusiastically and be . . . good by scholarly standards . . .

STEP 7: GOOD HOUSEKEEPING

Encourage setting up the material on the cart so that things can easily be located and used. In the process of sorting and filing, the students will be doing much of their best learning.

STEP 8: MAKING THE SOUND-SLIDE UNITS

On the whole, we think the first sound-slide unit, which should be designed to show people how to use a cart effectively, should concentrate on a specific, sharply-focused subject. For example, the economic plight of the Indian today. The overview unit, which probably will be needed on any cart, should be put together last after the students have really mastered their material.

Hopefully, by this time there will be a team of several students working on the Lab-Cart who reinforce and encourage each other and share the research and planning.

Bear in mind that the sound-slide units are not designed simply to pour forth facts, but to guide others into their own inquiry patterns. For example, the economic unit in this case might well focus on how an economist thinks, rather than on current economic data, which rapidly become obsolete anyhow.

STEPS IN MAKING A SOUND-SLIDE UNIT

1. Draw up a rough outline.
2. Think how to best present ideas in picture form.
3. Make a story board.
4. Revise story board and outline . . . until everybody on the team is satisfied. You'll have some great arguments. . . . THAT'S WHAT LEARNING IS ALL ABOUT!
5. Make the slides.
6. Record the soundtrack. . . . the students will be nervous. . . . Let them do a lot of practicing. . . . LET THE KIDS PLAN THE MUSIC BACKGROUND—PREFERABLY USING THEIR OWN INSTRUMENTS FOR LIVE, ORIGINAL ACCOMPANIMENT.
7. Synchronize . . . if you can; if not, use a beep signal.
8. Make revisions as necessary.
9. Using this valuable body of experience, let them continue making sound-slide units so that all the material in the cart is covered in programmed sound-slide presentations. The Lab-Cart should provide both materials and a method for learning.
10. And away we go! . . . Get the unit into use—in the class, anybody's classes. Let the kids who created it put it into use.

In all these steps the teacher would do well to bear in mind the basic advice of one of the Laboratory's founders on the subject of Lab-Carts:

Lab-Carts work if the teacher lets the program belong to the kids. Lab-Carts fail if the teacher must be an "enabler," a resource specialist. He must *not* be a lecturer, a demander, a giver of wisdom.

In other words, one vital purpose in creating a Lab-Cart is to encourage the student to evaluate his own work and provide his own motivation as he seeks his own brand of wisdom. This does not imply that Lab-Carts ought to have sloppy academic standards—it means that students need encouragement in raising their own standards.

The Social Studies Laboratory at Enfield High School has been a success since the day it opened its doors. There are now about two hundred and fifty Enfield students, out of a student body of twelve hundred and fifty, using the Laboratory. Of these, perhaps fifty are devoted Lab assistants who spend many hours working on their own projects and providing technical or other assistance for the projects of other students. Perhaps another fifty are students who have decided to pursue an individual interest and are preparing a sound-slide show on their own initiative and on their own time without any school credit. Perhaps one hundred and fifty are students who have reached an agreement with a teacher, not just a social studies teacher, that, in exchange for a certain amount of class credit or time out from class, they will work on a Lab project that will be of interest to the rest of the class. These students fill the Laboratory at all hours of the school day and many hours after school. Some work on Living History Center Projects, some on Lab-Carts, some on more modest endeavors such as closed-circuit TV shows about Enfield High School events.

The Social Studies Laboratory is truly the students' own institution. The Lab has a faculty advisor—a social studies teacher—but the students really operate the program. Student administrators include a student-faculty board of directors, a student executive director, and two separate branches of administration for creative projects and support services, each of which is headed by a student director and staffed by individual project directors. These young people decide whether a student's proposal will be funded or not (most proposals are approved since the cost of film, tape, and books is usually not large), instruct him in the use of Lab equipment, offer suggestions as to how best to achieve certain effects, and keep after him if his project falls behind schedule and deprives other students of access to equipment. The student administrators are competent in their jobs and have the respect of their fellow-students.

Perhaps the most significant success achieved by the Social Studies Laboratory at Enfield High School is the way it has led students to a more mature and more useful understanding of what the learning process is all about. Lab workers have begun to see that "good" teachers are not all-knowing masters but are fellow searchers after knowledge. They begin to see that knowledge is not contained in pat answers and that true learning is a creative process, not a regurgitating of facts. As they begin to understand these things, students grow in self-confidence and self-motivation.

"In the end," said a faculty member about a student working on a Lab-Cart, "he has created something out of his own heart and mind that he can point to and say with pride, 'I did this—I created something that is unique and that will survive and grow after I have gone on to other things.' "

This assertion reflects perhaps the most important fact about the Social Studies Lab: a student does not feel that his "learning" is something to be written down as a report or in an examination to be read quickly by a teacher and then forgotten forever. Every project completed in the Lab is kept on tap—as part of a Lab-Cart, or in a slide bank, or on file. Nothing useful is thrown out. Every contribution remains available as a resource for other students, for teachers in their classes, and for the people of the town of Enfield.

Projects completed by students in the Social Studies Lab have been of significant use to all these different groups of people. Students often use the projects of other students as springboards for their own, and teachers constantly come to the Lab to borrow materials for their classrooms. Recently Lab products have been used by some teachers for nine-week mini-courses. One of these mini-courses is a study of the sea-bed and is an interdisciplinary experiment by biology and social studies classes. The Lab has generated increased respect for the students from Enfield High's administrators, and this increased respect has brought about greater official willingness to explore other forms of educational innovation. Furthermore, Enfield community groups have been stirred and impressed by many of the Lab's Living History Center projects. For example, "L.I.F.E.," a sound-slide presentation about pollution, has been screened by more than a dozen Enfield organizations.

Why has the Laboratory had such extraordinary success? Predictably enough, there is no single answer. In part, one would have to point to the freedom and independence students have as they work on a Lab project. There are deadlines and other rules, and there are fellow-students to enforce them, but the fundamental questions of what to study and how to study are left largely to each student. This provides great appeal as well as great learning potential. Many students thrive with the freedom to explore alternatives to term papers, routine tests, and the daily assignments that often seem to break the continuity of learning, particularly if the learning task is one that requires attention over a period of time.

Also important is the appeal to self-discipline and self-motivation. Most students like to feel that they are being trusted, that they are being treated as responsible people, and that they are being helpful to others. Many students want to get away from grades as a measure of success, and probably all students want to feel that they are being truly creative. The fact that the Lab-Carts preserve their contributions for others to use provides a sense of achievement and builds self-esteem.

There is also another very important reason why the Lab has been successful: students have many chances to experiment with film and tape. Young people of this generation are almost universally excited by the prospect of making films and tapes. They like the process of making them, and they are comfortable with the equipment that is used. They are more at home with films and tapes than previous generations have been, and they see the creative potential of these media. Undoubtedly the emphasis on audio-visual productions and the availability of cameras, tape recorders, slide projectors, and synchronizers have contributed enormously to the Lab's popularity and to the high quality of its output.

Despite the extensive use of film and tape in the Enfield Social Studies Laboratory, the Lab has been able to operate on a very low budget. This should be good news to school districts that might want to adopt an Enfield-type lab. High quality, long-lasting, basic audio-visual equipment is not prohibitively expensive. Furthermore, audio-visual equipment is already available in most of today's schools. The point is to use it! Use it more fully and in ways that have perhaps not been tried before, including making it accessible to students for creative uses. At Enfield, the student administrators have been consistently prudent and economical, and there is no reason to expect student administrators in other schools to act any less responsibly.

It has been the Enfield Lab's policy, stemming from an awareness that many innovative programs flounder when money for experimentation is no longer available, not to accept a special outside grant unless given some assurance by the Enfield Board of Education that the Board will continue to fund a project after the first grant is terminated. This policy has worked out very well. Eastman Kodak supplied initial equipment and the State of Connecticut supplied three small cash grants, but that is *all* the outside funding the program has received. The Enfield Board of Education, reflecting the town's respect for the program, now supplies the $1,000 per year on which the Lab survives.

But there can be problems other than money, and Enfield has had its share of them. For one thing, the Lab continues to be regarded skeptically by some social studies teachers. Most of the social studies teachers, along with many teachers from other departments, permit students to work on a class project in the Lab, but only a few social studies teachers regularly come into the Lab to work with their students on the projects. The potential for increased student-teacher rapport has thus been limited to a smaller number of students and teachers than is theoretically possible. In some cases, nonparticipation in the Lab is caused by disagreement with the Lab's way of teaching and learning, and it seems unlikely that this problem will be overcome quickly. Another problem, perhaps related partially to teacher skepticism, is the reluctance of some students to believe in their own potential, to believe that they can come into the Lab and really create something that other students will be interested in looking at and finding out about. This reluctance, in part the product of years of passivity in school, keeps some students away from the Lab; it also prevents some students, once they actually come into the Lab, from working as effectively as they otherwise might.

The Lab's faculty advisor is optimistic about resolving these problems. First of all, he believes that the self-doubts bred by years of passivity give the Lab a special mission. It will have done much for Enfield's students, he believes, if it can shake them out of their reticence and insecurity, if it can prove to them that they, like their teachers, are capable of having important and interesting thoughts and discovering effective ways to express them. Second, he believes that the reluctance of some teachers to come into the Lab has left the Lab's students with an especially strong feeling that the Lab is their own place—a feeling that has contributed significantly to a productive and lively spirit. The Lab's spirit is evident in these paragraphs from the *Creative Impulse*, the pamphlet that was one of the Lab's earliest major projects:

We're beginning to knock down the walls that we've complained about for years: the walls that separate teacher from student, school from the outside world, and subject matter from reality. We're beginning to knock down the walls of prejudice and habit, too—the old notions that bell-shaped curves, neatly lined-up desks and fancy plan books are signs of good teaching. We're challenging the stereotypes that nullify advance: the assumptions that reforms require big budgets, big name consultants, and big sums of money. We're challenging the bugaboo that educational progress has to come from high-powered universities and evaluations from national tests. We refuse to lie awake at night with old fears that if your students don't match other students in a standardized test, something is wrong with your teaching. Indeed, it may be evidence that something *right* is beginning to happen—that you are not turning out standardized human beings, but individuals.

This does not mean that we intend to throw the baby out with the bath—we value tradition when it is noble, uplifting, and has the capacity to enrich human life. We hope that our brand of education will make our students fight to preserve the best colonial buildings of their old New England town—and we hope that the same brand of education will make them fight just as hard to tear down our slums.

But in the song our youngsters sing, there's something "blowin' in the wind." It's a freshening breeze. . .

STUDENTS CONCERNED WITH PUBLIC HEALTH
PHILADELPHIA, PENNSYLVANIA

In 1968 the Education Services Director of the Philadelphia-Montgomery Tuberculosis and Health Association met with a group of students at Philadelphia's largely black Simon Gratz High School who were dissatisfied with their biology and health education classes. The students were impressed with the Director's ideas about health education and asked him to take part in another larger meeting. Students Concerned with Public Health developed out of this meeting. It began as an organization of thirty Simon Gratz students and one adult, all dedicated to developing their own health education materials and getting these materials into the hands of other students in Philadelphia's public schools.

From the very beginning, the students had the main voice in making the group's decisions. Their chief criticism of traditional health education was that it was presented in such complicated and unappealing terms (thick textbooks full of technical language) that many students just didn't "turn on" to health information that was actually of vital importance to them. The group, therefore, set about developing materials and techniques that would appeal to elementary school children. They presented information through posters, comic books, cartoon strips, puppet shows, and science experiments. They chose to emphasize health problems that would be most immediate and pressing for these students as they grew a little older—drug abuse, alcoholism, venereal disease, and tuberculosis. In addition, they began to think of ways in which they might encourage young children to think about embarking on health careers.

The Philadelphia-Montgomery Tuberculosis and Health Association agreed to sponsor the group and assigned its Education Services Director to help. Free office space was obtained from the Association, and the group began to hold meetings there several days a week during science class and after school.

Alcoholism was the first topic the students chose to tackle. They visited Philadelphia's Diagnostic and Rehabilitation Center and spent a day talking about the problem with physicians, psychologists, social workers, street workers, alcoholics, and ex-alcoholics. Then they visited Eagleville Hospital and

Rehabilitation Center to talk with the professional staff and observe group therapy in action. Next they met with people from the Delaware Valley Alcoholism Council. Finally, the Students Concerned group did extensive reading on the subject and began preparing their materials—a play, comic books, posters, and various puppet shows.

Members of the group then formed teams of three or four students and went out into the schools and playgrounds of North Philadelphia with their puppets, comic books, and plays to educate children about health problems and health careers. They worked mainly with fifth- and sixth-graders but in some instances they also worked with fourth-graders. Health careers were stressed as attainable and worthwhile goals that could give purpose to learning and provide an alternative to self-destructive behavior such as gang warring, alcohol or drug abuse, or dropping out of school.

The work of Students Concerned has expanded in ways that will be described a little later, but the student visits to elementary school children are still the heart of the program. A team, equipped with a well-worked out presentation based on their own material, is driven by a staff member of Students Concerned to the scheduled schools. Each team includes one or two experienced seniors who are assisted by one or two juniors or even sophomores who are in training for the following year. When they arrive at the school, the students put on white coats with SCPH on the pockets; this gives them both visibility and an air of authority. The children and some of their teachers will be waiting for them in an appropriate hall or classroom.

If the puppet theatre is to be used, it will be set up and a short explanatory speech will precede the play. The puppets, made by Students Concerned, consist of large styrofoam heads and small bodies and are fitted onto the hand. One original play on alcoholism shows two old friends meeting in a park. One is obviously an alcoholic, and the other is shocked

Heads carved out of styrofoam serve as puppets for a drama on alcoholism.   PETER KLEINBARD

to see how much his friend has deteriorated. The alcoholic talks about how badly life has treated him and then persuades his friend to go home with him. The scene changes to the home where the man's wife and son, both the victims of the father's excessive drinking, explain how alcohol has ruined their lives. The alcoholic tries to justify himself and begins shouting at the family. Eventually he gains insight and is persuaded by his family and his friend to accept his need for some kind of treatment. The family comes to realize that they are all involved in the alcoholic's problem and have their own role in his recovery.

When the show is over, the students come out from behind the theatre and begin a dialogue with the younger children. Questions are asked about what they have just seen: "Who knows what an alcoholic is?" "A man with red eyes," says one young boy. The questioner points out that red eyes can come from different causes and that people who aren't alcoholics sometimes have red eyes. "What would you do if you knew someone who had an alcoholism problem?" another questioner asks. A hand shoots up: "I know someone—my dad." And so it goes.

The materials on drug abuse emphasize that everyone "turns on" in one way or another. Some turn on with drugs or alcohol; some turn on through productive work and human relationships. The students then point out that the first kind of "turning on" is artificial and that it is often a cowardly way out. Productive work in public health or medicine, for example, is a better alternative. And taking drugs is *not* a "hip" thing to do!

As the Students Concerned program developed and gave evidence of filling a real need, it began to gain recognition and support. A former Surgeon General of the United States took an interest in the group and arranged an informal meeting with the students and interested professionals at the Temple University Skin and Cancer Hospital. As a result of this meeting, the area Neighborhood Youth Corps (NYC) office became aware of the project and began to become involved with it. Most of the original Students Concerned members were eligible for enrollment in NYC and were put on its payroll for twelve hours per week. The following summer NYC extended the number of hours per week for which it would pay to thirty-two. Most Students Concerned put in many extra, unpaid hours, and many students who served as unpaid volunteers worked as hard as those who received pay. Needless to say, the NYC affiliation gave Students Concerned a substantial boast.

An important contribution of the group's adult advisor has been to help students make a growing number of influential individuals and groups in Philadelphia aware of the need for reform in public school health education and to increase the city-wide visibility of Students Concerned. The students have been engaged in a twofold attack on the problem of health education: (1) they are providing relevant and appealing health education and (2) at the same time they are helping to create a climate for change in health education programs—possibly in the direction of a large-scale replication of their efforts.

Students Concerned with Public Health is an active and expanding program. More than one hundred students participate during the school year, and slightly more than that work in a summer program. Students Concerned reached nine thousand Philadelphia school children (grades four through six) in the 1971–72 school year, averaging three visits per class. In the early part of the 1972–73 school year, they were teaching four thousand children a month. The first "class" of Students Concerned has graduated, but before they left high school, they recruited a new and interested group of youngsters just leaving junior high school.

Other developments are taking place as the program gains increasing acceptance. No longer are the participants almost all black, and no longer do they come exclusively from Simon Gratz High School. Saint Maria Goretti High School, a Catholic girls school in South Philadelphia, now has Students Concerned among its ranks, and young people from the Akiba Hebrew Academy outside of Philadelphia are also involved. In all, SCPH now has members from seven area high schools.

The organization continually expands the range of its activities. Its members have made numerous trips around the country to speak, for example, at annual meetings of the American Public Health Association and at the most recent White House Conference on Children.

A member of Students Concerned became the first student to be elected to Philadelphia's prestigious ninety-four-year-old Citizens' Committee on Public Education.

In April 1970, Students Concerned cosponsored a Health Happening at Philadelphia General Hospital. Teenagers went there to meet socially committed medical leaders and to gain a basic understanding about the interrelationships of medical, social, economic, and psychological problems. This Health Happening was followed by similar and equally successful events.

In conjunction with WPHL-TV they helped to develop a series of six television shows in which local experts discussed issues related to human growth and development and also described how childhood experiences can relate to later health problems such as alcoholism and drug abuse.

Surveys conducted by Students Concerned suggest that their programs have had a substantial and positive effect on elementary school children by engaging their interest in both health problems and health careers. In the materials on health careers, the opportunities for meeting a very important community need and for finding self-fulfillment at the same time are emphasized.

Of equal importance, and perhaps more immediately observable, is the impact the program has on the Students Concerned themselves. For example, students of different races work together as cooperating, mutually respecting equals, recognizing that the object of their concern—poor health— is no respecter of race or color. Also, they have gained confidence and skill in working with adults as they have had to deal with them to obtain certain kinds of support and help. They are learning, in effect, how to get things done. Finally, because they are themselves living the advice they offer the elementary school girls and boys—pursuing health careers and community service as an alternative to the artificial turn-on of drugs, for example—Students Concerned are free from some of the most serious health problems and are ready to face promising futures.

Students Concerned say proudly that every graduate of the program has been accepted by a college and offered financial aid, but not all have been able to take advantage of the opportunity for continuing study. Several members of Students Concerned have switched from general to academic programs so they can pursue a degree in nursing, medicine, medical social work, biochemistry, or health education. Some are contemplating the study of marine biology in recognition of the fact that the oceans seem now to be the greatest future source of human food and the greatest hope for relieving nutritional deficiencies.

Students Concerned with Public Health operates on a tight budget. Originally the Diagnostic and Rehabilitation Center provided a salary for the adult advisor, and the City Health Department provided health professionals from its staff to help train the high school students. The Health Department continues to provide training help to supplement efforts of other agencies and individuals.

The Neighborhood Youth Corps still provides funds to pay salaries to some Students Concerned, but the majority of student workers are volunteers. Prospective candidates for SCPH are told of the possibility of a paying job, but no promises are made; all students who participate are truly interested in the program.

All in all, there are enough funds available to maintain an office, provide some transportation, and pay for administrative help. The one major financial problem—in fact, perhaps the only major problem the program has—is adequate transportation under appropriate supervision. The gang situation in Philadelphia is so serious that the student advisor will not permit members of Students Concerned to use public transportation or to walk around strange neighborhoods. Private transportation is needed, and there isn't enough money to pay for an adequate number of cars and drivers.

No one in the program seems to mind the shortage of money, however. On the contrary, they may derive some satisfaction from it. The students feel that this is really their program. They know that their efforts are essential to keep it going, and they feel at home in the crowded, hectic, but friendly environment in which they work.

Students Concerned have a good relationship with the Board of Education. Perhaps the schools' most important contribution is permitting Students Concerned to go into elementary school classrooms and work with young children on health problems.

One reason for the success of the program is the eminent good sense of the idea itself. But there are other reasons, and these should be given close consideration by school administrators or others who consider establishing a similar program:

☐ Students work in two directions at the same time: (1) they teach younger students and (2) they also work for change in the adult political system by serving on health committees, keeping in contact with adults involved in health problems and programs, writing position papers on controversial health issues, and the like.

☐ The agency is almost totally student run and student organized. Policy is made by the students and develops from their work. There is a kind of joyful abandon in the way the students try out ideas that crop up. Some ideas have failed—like the idea of taking materials to sick children in hospitals. The sick children were simply too ill to listen. But many ideas have succeeded through the sheer determination, audacity, and vitality of the Students Concerned.

☐ Students Concerned realize that the program's emphasis must be on *community* health, and this means it cuts across racial and socio-economic lines. Students from different backgrounds are working together on a common problem.

☐ The need to operate on some sort of schedule and the emphasis on personal commitment have produced an atmosphere of responsibility, even though there is a great deal of informality and a somewhat "loose" organization in the administration of the program.

☐ There is an atmosphere of selflessness. This is not a program for *our* neighborhood, *our* school; the students are ready to help everybody, convert everybody, go anywhere. They want to "get through" to people of all ages. Equally or perhaps more important is their determination to be responsible, as citizens, for working to see that policy is changed in the ways they think it should be and their willingness to work within the establishment to bring about needed change.

The self-confidence of the members may also be viewed as a manifestation of good health in the broad way that Students Concerned wish to define it. The following statement of principle and fact, prepared by Students Concerned, supports this concept:

It is the philosophy of the Students Concerned and our director that only with . . . understanding of the structure, institutions, leaders and problems of society can the students truly become worthwhile citizens working within the establishment for constructive change. We further believe that once a person can learn the skills and frustration tolerance to work within the system for necessary change, they will not turn to the artificial world of drugs because they will see themselves as having human worth and of being needed by others and obtain the rewards that come from knowing you are dedicated to working for good. There is not one member of SCPH who uses drugs, and we would know if any of us did because our relationships are very close. We consider ourselves to be proof that young people will not turn to drugs if they see themselves as having unique abilities that can be used to serve others.

Finally, it should be noted that the director of Students Concerned has been an extremely important factor in the program's success. The adult advisor is a person who has tremendous faith in young people, enormous energy, imagination, willingness to take risks, and an openness to change and experimentation.

EDUCAGE
WHITE PLAINS, NEW YORK

Educage is a school for dropouts that is cosponsored by the Cage Teen Center and the White Plains, New York, Board of Education. It is an offshoot of The Cage, a neighborhood hangout where young people can obtain help with drug problems or simply get together to talk.

In 1967 several of the teenagers indicated that they wanted to complete their high school education. The Cage's director, a former guidance counselor and high school teacher, responded by offering remedial classes. He then asked the White Plains Board of Education to allow credit for courses taken at Educage. The Board agreed, and Educage became a school in its own right. In this school for dropouts, teachers and students decide what will be included in the curriculum, thus helping to assure that the courses will be dynamic and relevant.

Today, housed in a local church, Educage serves one hundred and twenty-eight students with another one hundred on a waiting list. Courses are diverse indeed: flying, video-mime photography, American history, reading, mathematics, psychology, cooking, typing, and sewing, for instance. The courses are taught by certified teachers, by secretaries, local businessmen, college professors, and housewives.

Each of twenty-two school districts pays a specified sum per year for each student it sends to Educage; an additional sum is given to the school each year by a local bank.

The informal atmosphere and the mutually respectful attitudes of students and teachers help make it possible for students to have a large measure of involvement in the day-to-day affairs of the school, including setting up courses, discussing discipline problems, and evaluating class work. Although they have no formal role in the administrative decision-making (the Board of Directors consists of businessmen and prominent citizens), students exhibit an extraordinary sense that the program is *theirs*.

Educage students dropped out of their regular high schools for a variety of academic and personal reasons. Some of them are young mothers whose education was interrupted by pregnancy. Others have been referred to Educage by courts or by schools. A day care center provides baby-sitting services while mothers take Educage classes. Most recently a residence was opened where as many as ten boys can live until difficulties with their families can be reconciled and they can return to their homes.

OTHER PROGRAMS

There are many other possibilities for students to become involved effectively in curriculum building. Some of these possibilities are developing outside the school system; some within it. Some of the programs are large scale; some small. Some projects that originate outside a school system ultimately become part of an ongoing school program; others do not—and they are perhaps more effective as alternatives to education that goes on within an institutionalized school system. Some alternative schools begin operation within the framework of an established school system and are later picked up by another school within the system and adapted as needed. In most of the alternative schools and in alternatives *to* school, young people have a significant part in planning and developing the program.

The possibilities are literally endless and a few—a *very* few —of the programs in which youth are involved in a curriculum-building capacity are described in the remainder of this chapter:

☐ The Elementary Institute of Science, Inc., is a private organization in San Diego, California, that seeks to interest young people in science, particularly young people from minority groups. It began its activities with a science fair, which has now become a yearly event for the San Diego schools. Each year students prepare projects and exhibits, and young people come from all over the city to observe and to learn from their fellow students' work.

The Institute was originally incorporated as an agency for children of elementary school age, but its range of activities has expanded to include high school students. In the summer, for example, high school students work on science projects that interest them. Another interesting development has been the establishment of internship programs that provide opportunities for high school students to work with scientists.

☐ The Museum of the Hudson Highlands, in Cornwall-on-Hudson, New York, is a museum of live animals and natural history. Its primary purpose is to interest young people in science, and it is run almost entirely by young people from nearby communities.

☐ The Youth Councils of the Oklahomans for Indian Opportunity seek to make young people aware of their Indian culture. They feel they are most successful when young people themselves search out traditional customs, stories, and skills and teach them to others.

☐ The High School Action-Research Project was a demonstration-type program developed by the Education and Training Association of New Haven, Connecticut, for disadvantaged, poorly performing students in the New Haven and Boston schools. It provided important opportunities to do research (surveys, interviews, and the like—particularly about how their own schools are run) and then to report their research findings, by oral or graphic means, to the other students in the Project.

☐ The Clinton Program is an alternative to regular school and is sponsored by the New York City Board of Education. Morning classes in basic academic skills are held at a youth center, and afternoon classes in "relevant" subjects, ranging from cooking to computers, are held at such places as television stations and stockbrokers' firms. Students help plan both their morning and their afternoon classes.

☐ At the Metro School, the Chicago Board of Education's "school without walls" where students use the facilities of the city as classrooms, it has been found that students respond especially well to units of study where they feel that they can make a unique personal contribution to a group investigation or project. At Metro, and elsewhere as well, when a student feels he is being counted on by his group, he tends to work harder than he otherwise might.

☐ Project Self of the Lord Byng Secondary School in Vancouver, British Columbia, has taken advantage of the phenomenon mentioned in connection with Metro. Project Self is an independent learning program. A student's independent project often revolves around a core curriculum that was arrived at only after lengthy student-faculty meetings devoted to the question, "What should be learned?" At these meetings, and in class discussions, a student often contributes the fruits of his independent project on one of the core topics.

☐ The Student Coalition for Relevant Sex Education began in 1971 when a group of New York City high school students, working with Planned Parenthood, determined to make useful sex education courses part of the school curriculum. The group's leader felt that, "We have seen too many of our classmates disappear during this school year because they had no alternative but to drop out and go on welfare to support their babies." Feeling that ignorance by young people is a large part of the problem, the group has succeeded in convincing the Board of Education to allow them to distribute information containing facts about human sexuality and to encourage interested teachers to include more useful information in ongoing health classes.

A FURTHER WORD

As has been indicated many times in this chapter, there are infinite ways in which students can participate in planning curriculum programs, help to develop them, and help to operate them. In probably every area of learning, young people have a positive contribution to make to some aspect of curriculum building. As it becomes increasingly clear how much educational benefit can accrue to students who have a chance to be curriculum builders, opportunities for them to play this dynamic teaching-learning role should multiply.

YOUTH
as teachers

The tutors benefit because working with a child, you never know what he is going to say. You can learn by listening. And they benefit because they have to know a lot themselves. In order to tutor, I had to learn to read better and be able to answer questions. You feel badly if a child asks you questions and you can't answer. And most young people like kids. All you really need is a place.

I don't think there's any comparison between this and the schools. I think this situation is better. Here the children get a one-to-one relationship. In school a teacher gets thirty-five children. A teacher doesn't get a chance to help each child.

What I'm doing is hard. First of all, you're working not only with young children but with kids your own age—now and then that's a problem. If you don't push your power around, you do all right but you let them know what you expect. I believe that these tutors do a good job and that anyone can do an effective job if they are doing what they want to do because they want to do it.

These statements were made by sixteen-year-olds who are teaching younger children at tutoring centers throughout the United States. The idea that there is something valuable in store for all students when they teach each other is not new. In the first century, the celebrated teacher Quintilian wrote about how much younger children in a school can learn from their older classmates. Some centuries later, in 1632, the Moravian teacher John Comenius supported the idea that the one who teaches may learn as much as, or more, than the person he teaches. Comenius wrote:

The saying, "He who teaches others, teaches himself," is very true, not only because constant repetition impresses a fact indelibly on the mind, but because the process of teaching in itself gives a deeper insight into the subject taught. . . . The gifted Joachim Fortius used to say that . . . if a student wished to make progress, he should arrange to give lessons daily in the subjects which he was studying, even if he had to hire his pupils.

For many years, in different parts of the world and in different situations, students have taught one another. Teaching each other was a regular feature of ancient Hindu schools. In the United States some of the earliest instances of students teaching students occurred at the time when public education was not universally available nor even universally desired. For children whose parents valued education and had the means to provide it, there were private tutors or private schools. For children whose parents felt that formal schooling was a waste of time, there was what their parents regarded as practical education—learning a trade as an apprentice, working on the family farm, or learning how to cook and clean and sew.

There were many parents, however, who wanted their children to have an education but did not have enough money to pay for it. And there were other people who realized that much talent would be wasted and much potential leadership would never be developed, if children were deprived of education simply because they came from poor families. One of these people was Joseph Lancaster, a Quaker from England.

In 1798 Lancaster opened a school for children from poor families. Because he could not afford to hire enough teachers to provide the individualized instruction he wanted for his students, he set up what he called the "monitorial system." This was a system of mutual education in which students "monitored" the instruction of other students with some adult supervision. This system proved to be such an effective learning device that Lancaster became a strong advocate of it as a desirable way to educate young people. Through his efforts and the efforts of Andrew Bell, a contemporary who adopted Lancaster's idea, the practice of students teaching students became very prevalent and remained popular for thirty years.

Then the system fell into disrepute, not because the basic idea was educationally unsound but because it was misused—particularly by opportunists who were more concerned with making money than they were with educating young people. They saw the economic advantages of reducing the number of paid teaching staff by using unpaid students as teachers, and for this economic advantage they were ready to sacrifice the instructional advantages of a tutorial system operated under the guidance of an adequate number of competent adult teachers. The predictable result—a decrease in student achievement—was incorrectly attributed to the tutorial system idea itself, and the idea was discredited and discarded.

In the 1960s a resurgence of interest in children teaching children occurred. The reasons for this renewed interest were numerous: the need for more individualized instruction than was possible for teachers to provide in large classes; the expectation that students would benefit greatly from their involvement in such teaching programs; the need and the demand for more relevant curricula; and concern about the number of young people who were dropping out of school.

Many experiments were conducted, and the values to be derived from students teaching students were again acclaimed.

Some of the most interesting experiments were carried out by Peggy and Ronald Lippitt. They paired older children with younger children in a number of different tutorial programs and sought to measure gains in the acquisition of knowledge and gains that fall roughly under the heading of "socialization." The Lippitts began their experiments tentatively believing in the following propositions:

Much of the process of socialization involves use by younger children of the behavior and attitudes of older children as models for their own behavior. This process has great potentiality for planned development as an effective educational force, provided that children are trained appropriately for their role as socialization agents.

Involvement of older children in a collaborative program with adults to help younger children will have a significant socialization impact on the older children because of (*1*) the important motivational value of a trust- and responsibility-taking relationship with adults around a significant task, and (*2*) the opportunity to work through—with awareness but at a safe emotional distance—some of their own problems of relationships with their siblings and peers.

Assisting in a teaching function will help the "teaching students" to test and develop their own knowledge, and also help them discover the significance of that knowledge.

Both younger learners and their adult teachers will be significantly helped in "academic" learning activities through the utilization of older children.

A child will develop a more realistic sense of his own ability and present state of development . . . if he has an opportunity to help children younger than himself to acquire skills which he already possesses.[1]

---

1. Peggy Lippitt and John E. Lohman, "Cross-Age Relationships—An Educational Resource," *Children*, vol. 12, no. 3, May-June 1965, pp. 113–17.

A major experiment conducted in the Detroit public schools involved sixty-eight students of high school, junior high school, and elementary school age. Older students, meeting with younger students in half-hour sessions three or four times a week, helped with a wide variety of skills—carpentry, spelling, sewing, and many others. Teachers reported that nearly all of the children involved—those who tutored (tutors) and those who were tutored (tutees)—showed academic gains that could be attributed to the program. Most of the children also showed socialization gains: "greater class participation, greater effort, extra work being done, better attendance, greater attentiveness, less fooling around, greater ability to express oneself, increased willingness to accept help, and greater self-confidence, self-respect, and self-image." The additional effects on the tutors were equally impressive: two-thirds of them said that their attitude toward school had improved, and three-fourths or more said they thought they understood other people better, were more considerate of others, and had greater self-confidence as a result of the tutoring program.

In the following pages several programs in which students function as teachers are described in fuller detail.

STUDENT CURRICULUM EXPERIENCE PROGRAM (SCEP)
PETALUMA, CALIFORNIA

Petaluma is a white, middle-class, suburban (almost rural) community forty miles north of San Francisco. No urgent needs nor strident demands required Petaluma to use its students in the role of teachers. Petaluma was free to develop a wide-ranging program, designed not so much to test whether a specific teaching role for students could remedy a specific dire problem, but rather to test a variety of possible ways in which students, acting as teachers, might enhance an educational program that was already reasonably satisfactory. Petaluma could, in fact, afford the luxury of experimentation.

The exercise of that luxury is apparent in Petaluma's rationale for the program that developed. It cites the conditions and needs that led to the program's development: the abundance of human resources that students represent; the common observation that students learn by teaching others; the dynamic quality of learning that young students sometimes experience when peers are their teachers; the contribution that students can make to "more relevant" curricula; the need to make maximum use of the skills of certified teachers by freeing them from tasks students can perform; the importance of demonstrating to teachers that some of their responsibilities can be shared successfully with students; the need to recruit young people into teaching; and the need to save money.

These conditions and needs run the gamut of all the rationales that have been commonly used for admitting students into teaching roles. Out of these conditions and needs, Petaluma developed a program of unusual boldness in which selected students were given full authority to conduct regular, full-credit, high school courses during the school day.

SCEP began operation at the two high schools of the Petaluma School District during the 1970–71 school year. The basic outline of the program was this: pairs of students, working together, taught regular full-credit seminars that they themselves had planned and developed. After head counselors, principals, and the superintendent of schools had discussed this basic outline, guidance counselors at Petaluma Senior High School and Rancho Cotate Senior High School were instructed to survey students for candidates for the teaching positions.

By November 10, 1970, six student leaders at Petaluma High, six at Rancho Cotate, and two at Homestead High School in the Fremont district had been selected. Expressed interest in the project was the first qualification for a prospective teacher. No specific preference was given to students who said that they hoped some day to become regular teachers. Of those expressing interest, seniors were given priority over students in lower grades. Finally, candidates were evaluated according to their apparent ability to do the job and according to a not-too-rigorous standard of financial need.

Only after their selection were the student leaders asked what it was they wanted to teach. Then they formed themselves into teams of two and began to develop courses, trying to reconcile their personal interests with what they interpreted to be the interests of their prospective students. Their course selections were as follows:

Petaluma High School
 United States: Current Issues and Problems
 United States: Current Cultural Concerns
 Africa: Current Problems and Issues

Rancho Cotate Senior High School
 Composition and Current Writing Styles
 Speed Reading
 Computer Applications

Homestead High School
 Introduction to Algebra

It was gratifying to SCEP's founders to observe the spread of the courses: three in social studies, two in English, and two in mathematics. Moreover, it seemed significant to them that all the courses emphasized *current* trends or applictions.

From mid-November 1970 until the end of January 1971, the student leaders worked hard planning their courses, gathering their materials, and meeting with their staff advisors —teachers in the relevant subject area who volunteered to assist on the project. Registration for the student-led classes opened in January. Speed Reading and Computer Applications were the first to fill up, but by the end of the month enrollment for all the courses was closed. The maximum number of students per course was twenty; the range was between fifteen and twenty.

All the courses proceeded smoothly throughout the second semester. They met on the same basis as other courses in their respective high schools, except that each class had a pair of teachers, rather than a single teacher. Full credit was granted to both the enrollees and the student leaders. In addition, the student leaders were paid for seven hours per week of outside-school preparation. Funds for these payments came from two sources: Sonoma County's federally-supported Work-Study Program and the Rosenberg Foundation of San Francisco. The Rosenberg grant also provided each seminar a specific sum for instructional materials. No supplementary salaries were paid to any of the project's faculty advisors who met with the student leaders regularly once a week, made occasional classroom visits, and were available for consultation nearly all the time.

At the end of the semester, numerous surveys were conducted of those who had been involved with or exposed to SCEP. For example the entire student bodies of Petaluma (fifteen hundred students) and Rancho Cotate (one thousand students) Senior High Schools were asked whether they had heard of the student-led courses and whether they would be interested in taking such a course. Of the fifty-one percent who replied, substantially more students who had heard about the program expressed an interest in taking a course than did students who had never heard of SCEP. Nearly two hundred students said they might like to be one of the student leaders.

The faculties of Petaluma and Rancho Cotate were similarly surveyed. Approximately three-fifths of the staff of fifty-six replied, and a full eighty-five percent of them asserted unequivocally that they would like to see their schools continue to offer student-led courses. Seventy percent said that they might be willing to serve as advisors to student seminar leaders.

The student leaders themselves, in response to a request for their reactions to the program made many thoughtful comments. Patty, who worked with Sue on United States: Current Cultural Concerns, said:

. . . I sometimes am annoyed that Sue and I can't get together and really plan what is going to happen. This is very difficult since Sue tends to be a very liberal teacher (no quizzes, little homework, etc.), and I am more conservative (assignments, etc.). I feel that the team partners must first make an agreement (before attempting to conduct a class of this nature) to cooperate with each other. Sue and I like each other but we have some barriers in the classroom. We were not thoroughly prepared for this undertaking—didn't understand each other's philosophy about teaching. This has been a major problem as far as having the class run smoothly . . .

Good points: I've had much experience—I know what to expect if I do decide to teach after college (which I most likely will do). I'm certain that the class has a better insight into the ideas and philosophies of other human beings. They seem more willing to listen to each other and work from that point forward. This was one of our basic goals. Many facts about different cultural concerns have been brought forth. . . .

Advisors had high praise for the program:

[The] standards of academic achievement [of the student leaders of the Petaluma High social studies seminars] have been high; but their classes are conducted openly so that discussion is not only factual but also many-sided. As a social studies teacher myself, I cannot find a higher reason for praise than this. I saw evidence of the strategies of [several student leaders]. Reflective thinking and value-laden discussion led to some rather logical conclusions in these classes.

There was also significant evidence that the enrolled students, as well as the students who taught the courses, grew and learned. One student in the class conducted by Patty and Sue had this to say:

... At first everyone was talking and nobody was listening. There was really no progress. But then compromise came into the picture, and though everyone didn't agree all the time, we would compromise and work out the solution. We succeded [in doing] on a small scale plan what countries have been trying to do. It opened me up to express my views and respect others. . . .

Another offered this comment:

... We have been able to express our beliefs and convictions with words; it isn't easy to, sometimes. We as a class have learned to look at classmates with individual backgrounds and personalities. We have learned a little patience and respect for differing opinions. . . .

No severe problems developed during the 1970–71 operation of SCEP. Occasionally a faculty advisor had to intervene to discipline a student. Occasionally, some teachers felt, there were problems in teaching methods such as student leaders deferring too much to the wishes of the class, pacing the class too slow, or letting the class become too "bookish" in imitation of the ways they themselves had been taught. These are teaching problems that are common throughout the profession, and it did not surprise or disturb anybody when they occasionally cropped up in the SCEP classes.

Of greater concern to SCEP's director is the future of the program. SCEP has continued to operate but on a reduced scale. The Rosenberg Foundation grant has expired, and the school budget has suffered cuts, but what is an even greater difficulty is a severe space shortage at the Petaluma high schools. The space problem is more serious than the money problem because Petaluma has found that wages are not really an essential part of the SCEP program. So long as a certain basic amount of money for supplies continues to be available, the program should survive financially.

The permanent solution hoped for by SCEP's director is that student-led courses, with a pattern of one master teacher, two pairs of student leaders, and two seminars of fifteen to twenty students each, will become part of the regular curriculum of the Petaluma schools. If this is done, the student leader program will be better able to compete for the district's funds and plant facilities; it will also have the district's good will and concern. Only by such incorporation is it likely that SCEP will be able to continue to expand and to realize the full potentialities of students in the role of teachers.

Whatever its future may be, SCEP can point to some very significant achievements. SCEP has shown that:

☐ Students can responsibly take charge of a regular high school classroom.

☐ Students in the role of teachers can successfully introduce new curricula into a high school program.

☐ Students in a class run by other students can achieve both academic and socialization growth.

☐ Students in the role of teachers can convince adult faculty members—including those who may initially be skeptical— that students *can be* effective instructional leaders.

BILINGUAL TUTORING PROJECT
RICHMOND, CALIFORNIA

Richmond, California, located twenty miles northeast of San Francisco and south of Petaluma, is a far different place from Petaluma. Richmond is an industrial community with sizeable and growing Mexican-American and black minorities. The school district must cope with student indifference, under-achievement, vandalism, drug abuse, and a score of other serious consequences and/or concomitants of poverty—and it must do this on a tight budget.

For some time, the plight of the Mexican-American community in Richmond has been an articulated concern of the Chicanos who attend the Contra Costa Junior College nearby. They have felt that it is a culturally submerged community, politically overwhelmed by the larger black community that surrounds it. They have felt that blacks and Chicanos are being made to fight over the same bone and that, in the face of limited government concern, blacks and Chicanos should work together, learning to respect and understand both the points at which their cultural and economic needs converge and the points at which they diverge. During late 1968 and early 1969, the concern of these teenage Chicanos focused on the needs of the younger children who were about to enter or had recently entered the Richmond elementary schools. Many of these children, part of a continuing stream of immigration, had only recently arrived with their families from Mexico; many others had spent all their growing-up years in Richmond homes where Spanish was the primary language. They were ill-equipped to enter schools where English was the language of instruction, and they immediately fell behind their classmates because they simply could not understand what was being taught. Their inability to understand provoked the development of psychological problems, for instance, insecurity and withdrawal, that further impeded the learning process. The problems were evident, but the Richmond School District was not able to provide the special services and facilities these children needed.

The older Chicano youth realized that the situation, if not remedied, would have serious effects on the whole next generation of Richmond's Chicano community, and they decided to do something about it. Their leader was a young man who had grown up in a well-assimilated working class family. In his early years he had not been particularly aware of his Chicano heritage nor particularly sensitive to the problems of many Chicanos, but his attitudes changed when, in college, he encountered the Third World Movement.

Under the leadership of this young man, a concerned group of Chicano youth developed some ideas of what might be done. They took their suggestions first to Richmond's United Council of Spanish-speaking Organizations and then to the Richmond School District. It took time, and it took the enthusiastic support of some sympathetic administrators, but eventually the School District approved the establishment of a bilingual tutoring project to be operated by the young proposers in conjunction with Lincoln School, an elementary school where twenty-five percent of the students were Chicano. For the 1970–71 school year, ESEA Title I funds were allotted to the project.

The design of the project was quite simple. Thirty children, half of whom had just entered kindergarten, received special instruction individually and as a group. They were tutored individually for an hour and half after school. Most of this tutoring took place in the homes. In addition, every Saturday afternoon they met as a group for further instruction.

There were ten tutors, each one in charge of three pupils. The tutors were local high school and junior college students —mostly Chicanos but a few of Anglo-Saxon descent. Almost all of them were bilingual, and all tutors were paid by the hour for their tutoring services. No one was paid less than the minimum wage; some received increments based on certain established criteria. In addition to the hours they spent with their pupils, the tutors attended staff meetings on Saturday mornings preceding the group classes. The Richmond School District assigned one credentialed teacher to serve as advisor to the group, and he worked directly with the young college student who initiated the project.

Instruction was intended to provide help in both academic

A member of the Bilingual Tutoring Project meets Chicano children at their home to take them to a tutoring session.
PETER KLEINBARD

and cultural areas. Academic help was not strictly confined to language skills, but such exercises as writing the alphabet and learning to pronounce words certainly predominated. The program's cultural aims were quite complex: for example, to provide knowledge of the way Christmas is celebrated in most homes in North America and at the same time to keep children sensitive to their Chicano heritage. This was in accordance with the belief that familiarity with some of the best in both cultures would help to build a lasting self-confidence in the child. It was in this need to build self-confidence that tutors recognized as the point at which the academic and cultural components of their program came together. With self-confidence these young children would learn in school; without it, they would not. As one way of developing confidence, exposure to language skills and cultural awareness were combined whenever possible.

This project, like many others, had its own particular problems. Some were sheer physical problems. For example, the children's homes were often noisy and crowded—not at all conducive to serious, attentive attitudes during the tutoring session. To remedy that situation, tutors went to some homes to meet their students and took them to a quiet corner of the Richmond library for a work session.

There were personnel problems, too—some relating to the tutors, some to adult supervision. Here again, the problems were not unlike difficulties in other projects, but in this particular situation, the presence of these problems influenced a later decision to change the nature of the program.

The project also had to cope with a certain amount of skepticism and distrust. For example, there were a few parents who were distrustful because the only classrooms they had ever known were the traditional, conservative ones of their Mexican youth with strict discipline and a rigidly prescribed academic course of study. These parents, understandably, found it hard to believe that the enthusiastic sessions of storytelling and finger painting could truly result in learning.

A few other parents were distrustful because their religious background had taught them to be skeptical of anything that seemed to them to stress "worldly" advancement.

Skepticism and distrust were also evident among some members of the school district's personnel. There were those who had doubts about any educational programs that went on outside the school's direct control and supervision. There were a few others who were uneasy because they mistook some of the program's modest efforts to build Chicano pride —such as showing a film about Cesar Chavez, the labor leader—for radical political education.

Nevertheless, during this first year, the Bilingual Tutoring Project could point to a number of significant accomplishments. Tests conducted before and after the project's operations showed that tutees had made substantial progress in the language arts, and the project's tutors felt justified in believing that at least some of that progress was attributable to their efforts. Moreover, tutors observed a blossoming of personality and a coming forth out of withdrawal that seemed to augur well for the learning prospects of these children.

As the year went by, most of the parents began to see the values this project offered for their children and started to support the project in ways that seemed likely to be important for long-term success. The skeptics in the school system were not so easily persuaded, and they insisted that the Bilingual Tutoring Project be brought directly into the Lincoln School under the supervision of the Lincoln faculty. For only one year, therefore, was the Bilingual Tutorial Project operated entirely by young people.

It is too early to say whether the project that now exists is as good a program as the Bilingual Tutoring Project that was devised earlier. There can be no question, however, that it is different. In 1971–72 there were thirteen tutors, but only five of them were college students. The other eight tutors were parents. The tutors now come to the school building, and for an hour each day they work directly under the guidance of a classroom teacher to whom they are assigned. Each tutored child still receives one hour of instruction at home each week, but that instruction is under the direction of the classroom teacher. A teacher will say: "This child can't tell *p* from *q*" or "This child needs help with the number *5*." The tutor's work for the day is defined for him, and he follows instructions without much opportunity to exercise initiative.

The revised program is more immediately sensitive to academic achievement than was the earlier program, but it seems to be less responsive to the possibilities for affective growth on the part of students. The truth is, of course, that *both* problems must be solved if *either* is to be solved. The Chicano youth who organized the Bilingual Tutorial Project recognized this truth. If the school personnel who now administer the program also recognize it, some of the effective, easygoing incorporation of American and Chicano culture that characterized the project in its first year may find its way back. The presence of parents in some of the tutoring roles may help to facilitate this.

In any case, there seems to be little likelihood of returning to the original format of the project. But if Lincoln School administrators can bring the same enthusiasm, dedication, and inventiveness that its young Chicano founders originally invested in it, the program should have a bright and important future.

YOUTH TUTORING YOUTH
NATIONWIDE

I guess what Sammy needs to learn most is how to be responsible. It comes out in his problems with English and reading and skills like that. See, if he had responsibility he'd have learned those better by now. But he doesn't, so he needs the responsibility now. That's what I really try to teach him, even though the work we do is mostly writing, spelling, and reading exercises.

Mike, the "teacher" who said this, had just turned seventeen, and until a few months before he had been in trouble because he kept skipping classes at high school to work on his car. School was a drag, he thought, and he planned to drop out soon like most of his friends. But Mike decided to hold off for a while, mainly because a little third-grader named Sammy needed to learn responsibility, and Mike thought he could help him.

Mike and Sammy were brought together by a program called Youth Tutoring Youth (YTY).[2] In one of the many possible arrangements under this program, Mike spends forty-five minutes, four days a week, tutoring Sammy in language-related skills. He plans his own lessons, uses materials he makes up, and takes personal—and deserved—credit for much of Sammy's considerable progress. In the years since 1967 when YTY began, more and more young people have shared some version of Mike's and Sammy's experience. Today there are more than one thousand such programs in more than four hundred and fifty cities across the United States.

Youth Tutoring Youth was originated by the National Commission on Resources for Youth (NCRY), an independent, nonprofit organization. The design for the program grew out of the Commission's perception of what might be done to expand greatly the contribution that could be made by the Neighborhood Youth Corps (NYC), the federally-sponsored program that provides jobs for needy young people. The NYC was providing jobs, but it seemed to the Commission that too many of these were dull, dead-end positions not conducive to growth. Furthermore, NYC's requirement that workers be at

_____
2. Ibid., pp. 73–97 for a more detailed discussion of this program.

least sixteen years old prevented the Corps from helping many young people at a time when they needed it most—the years immediately preceding the age when they could drop out of school. If their interest could be captured then, their abilities challenged, and their self-esteem increased, the Commission felt that the chances of their dropping out of school might well be reduced.

The Commission proposed Youth Tutoring Youth as a source of NYC employment with real significance for teenagers. The proposal included a recommendation that the age of NYC eligibility for certain positions be lowered to fourteen. In response, the United States Department of Labor —NYC's sponsoring agency—funded two prototype YTY programs. Under NCRY administration the two programs operated in Newark, New Jersey, and Philadelphia, Pennsylvania, during the summer of 1967. Because they were both successful, and because they featured many elements that were copied in later YTY programs, it is worth examining these two pilot programs in some detail.

First, YTY's origin as a proposal to provide significant employment for youth has accounted for its predominating emphasis on the tutors as the program's chief beneficiaries. Benefits to the tutees have been regarded as a bonus. Furthermore, since one purpose of YTY was to forestall school dropouts, the program was aimed largely at underachievers as the ones who had the most to gain from tutoring.

Thus, the first two hundred tutors in the Newark and Philadelphia programs were all fourteen or fifteen years old and were all below their grade level in reading. The tutees were substantially younger than the tutors and were themselves underachievers. Tutors were paid the minimum hourly wage for twenty-two hours of work each week. Six of these hours were spent in training, and each tutor met each of his two tutees for two hours, four times a week. Tutors also spent six unpaid hours each week on remedial work.

The two programs had common goals: to show that fourteen- and fifteen-year-old underachievers could tutor still younger underachievers on a one-to-one basis with substantial benefit to tutors, tutees, the schools, and the community. In their respective structures and their operational details, however, the programs showed the kind of diversity that has become a hallmark of local YTY programs. In Philadelphia one hundred and twenty tutors were divided among six different schools; in Newark, eighty tutors were assigned to one school. In Philadelphia each of the six centers was directed by a credentialed teacher who was assisted by a NYC enrollee slightly older than the tutors. In Newark, on the other hand, the school's community was deeply involved in the program. A community committee helped recruit tutors and tutees and helped select six community persons to serve as the tutors' supervisors. The committee selected mothers and other residents, most of whom had never finished high school, and three of whom had led actions against the Board of Education.

Each center developed its own individual character: some centers used learning games extensively; some used the community as the prime learning resource; and a structured school environment was maintained in one. In both Newark and Philadelphia, however, the basic concern was for the tutors— their ability to teach and to learn through teaching.

By the end of the summer it was clear that the tutors had made substantial gains. Here are some of the observations:

☐   The care and excitement with which a tutor led a tutee through a challenging lesson, showing that once responsibility is given, it will be accepted and used with great benefit.

☐   The tutors' sustained interest and participation (only seven of the two hundred tutors left the program; some left because of illness, and some left for a higher paying job).

☐   The understanding and easy rapport that developed between tutor and tutee, demonstrating that tutors did identify with younger children.

☐ The influence their activities seemed to have in helping tutors work at their own problems—problems such as lack of self-confidence, lack of motivation, need for creative outlets, and need for respect and recognition.

☐ The new pride evident in the tutors as they grew in their new role of "teacher"—grew in their own eyes as well as in those of parents, teachers, and tutees.

☐ The books that were removed from shelves and circulated in the group as published works came into their lives in a real way for the first time.

☐ The endless variety of complex and simple materials they devised as their creativity thrived in their attempts to spur tutees.

☐ The new confidence that displayed itself in finding ways to communicate with the tutee in an individual relationship.

☐ The successful participation of subprofessional community people, and the enthusiasm and support these people engendered in others, many of them parents.

Gains were also measured in terms of standardized reading tests. Tutors were tested at the beginning of the summer and again at the end of the seven-week program. Philadelphia's tutors started the summer 0.4 grades behind their age level in reading and increased their mean reading age equivalency by one year. In Newark, where the tutors had begun the summer "behind" by 2.9 years, an extraordinary 3.5 years gain was recorded. It is, of course, most unlikely that the Newark tutors actually gained that much in so short a time. One possible explanation of the "gain" may lie in the effect that a student's attitude can have on his performance in a testing situation. If at the beginning of the summer students were negative—or even just indifferent—toward the reading tests, they may not have exerted themselves enough to provide a reasonably accurate measure of their ability. Later after several weeks in which they had been functioning as valued human beings, successfully helping younger people learn to

A high school student works with a younger boy on writing skills. BRUCE DOLLAR

read, they may well have lost their indifference and cared enough to do their very best. This in itself, the Commission believes, has important implications for education and for educators.

The highly favorable results of these two programs led NCRY to encourage widespread replication of Youth Tutoring Youth. Subsequent programs brought continued successes, the idea of YTY spread rapidly, and it would be impossible to say precisely how many successful projects are now in operation. By no means are all of them on record in NCRY files. But the Commission currently maintains correspondence with at least five hundred locations throughout the country, and in each of these communities there can be anywhere from ten to twenty, or even more, active projects.

To obtain further data on the effects of Youth Tutoring Youth in a cross-section of programs, NCRY commissioned a comprehensive evaluation research project. The formal research, completed in 1972, was carried out in programs in twenty schools in Chicago and eleven schools in Washington, D.C. In its report on tutors in these programs, the Social Psychology Laboratory at the University of Chicago found that tutors showed marked improvement in language skills, more positive self-image, and increased interest in going to school. Similar favorable results were recorded for tutees: they showed increased reading interests and skills, improved self-confidence, and better classroom behavior.

YTY has a number of unique qualities that have contributed to its expansion. One of these has been its ability to attract funding from a variety of agencies. Besides Neighborhood Youth Corps, which has continued as a source of funds for tutors, early financial support came from Title I of the Elementary and Secondary Education Act (ESEA), from the United States Office of Education's Career Opportunities Program (COP), and later from such sources as Model Cities, VISTA, Teachers Corps, school budgets, and private foundations. Furthermore, since NCRY's role, after the initial demonstrations, switched from administrator to advisor and facilitator, there has been no central authority to "enforce" any single design or set of procedures—a fact that has helped to foster many local variations of the basic concept.

Another feature of YTY that has helped further its expansion is its ready adaptability to a wide range of local conditions and needs. Having begun as a successful summer program, subsequent experience showed it could be equally effective during the school year as an after-school program or as an in-school program in which tutors receive high school credit for their work. Although YTY was originally designed for teenagers of drop-out age, there was no reason why the basic concept could not be applied to youngsters of any age. There are many places where junior high school students tutor elementary school children and older elementary school children teach younger children.

The basic concept of YTY can be applied to virtually any instructional area, and this is still another factor in the program's widespread popularity. Its adaptability to academic objectives and to other special needs of individual tutors or tutees helps account for its nearly limitless potential for local application.

To give an idea of the versatility all these combined features have given to YTY, here are some examples of variations on the basic theme:

☐ In Trinidad, Colorado, the program was operated almost completely by tutors. There was an administrator, but the elected officers among the tutors handled all the correspondence, the gathering of materials, and all the operational details usually assigned to an administrator. They contacted the press, and they helped recruit the tutees. . . .

☐ In Cleveland, Ohio, fatherless boys served as tutors in order that they might form a relationship with younger boys who were also fatherless. This project was designed as an after-school program in a particular school where there were a number of Aid to Dependent Children parents using foundation funds. The program concentrated on trying to build a good male relationship between the two groups of boys. . . .

☐ In two Indian villages in New Mexico, young tutors were used in a unique way. Since Pueblo is not a written language, and since the young do not ordinarily learn crafts, it is not likely that the tribe's crafts will be transmitted to another generation. Therefore, a plan was devised whereby teenage tutors taught a craft (and learned it while doing so) to younger children. This proved very successful, both for the tutors and the tutee. Pictures and slides of the children were sent to adjoining villages to encourage other Pueblo groups to develop similar "tutoring" programs. . . .

In light of the extraordinary diversity among the local versions of YTY, one might wonder what it is that distinguishes them as Youth Tutoring Youth. Rather than a common administrative structure or common curriculum content, these programs all share a set of principles—an approach or a philosophy concerning the specific people who are involved. This is in keeping with NCRY's belief that the critical elements in a program's success are human relationships and the atmosphere in which they take hold and flourish.

The principles have been developed over a time by the Commission in its role first as originator, then as trainer, advisor, and provider of informal technical assistance for a multitude of YTY programs across the country. Drawing on this experience, NCRY has produced manuals, guides, pamphlets, and films, which it has made available to prospective and actual program operators. These materials include *A Manual for Trainers, A Supervisor's Manual*, and a series of booklets called *For the Tutor, You're the Tutor*, and *Tutoring Tricks and Tips*.

The keystone of the entire YTY edifice is the conviction that an older child can capably tutor a younger child with certain tangible and predictable benefits for both. Underlying this, however, is a series of principles NCRY has found to be critical in assuring a successful demonstration of the central idea. Perhaps most important is the amount of responsibility accorded to the tutors, for YTY is also based on the belief, now proven through experience, that when older children are given the opportunity to make their own decisions about questions that matter to them, they *will* act responsibly and gain enormously from the experience.

Tutors are encouraged to take the initiative in deciding what and how to teach the tutee in their charge—within the limits prescribed by the program, of course. If the program is geared to language arts, for instance, it is up to the tutor to determine the specific needs of his tutee and to plan his lessons accordingly. This is what Mike did, as reflected in his comment at the beginning of this section. When Mike was first assigned to Sammy, all he was told was that Sammy was way behind in reading and needed lots of help. For their first real project together, after a period of getting acquainted, Mike bought Sammy a model car. It was his own idea and he used his own money. As Mike described it later:

First I read the directions to him and put it together while he watched. Then I took it apart again and said "Now you do it." So he had to read the directions to me first, which I helped him with, and then he followed them and put it together all by himself. It was the best thing we ever did together.

What made this "the best thing" Mike and Sammy ever did was the feeling of accomplishment and increased self-confidence that Mike got from knowing that he himself was responsible for the successful episode with Sammy. It established Mike as a competent tutor, in both his own eyes and in Sammy's, in a way that would not have been possible had Mike simply been carrying out an assignment from the supervisor "to teach him this."

Mike was permitted to decide not only what to teach Sammy but also what general approach to take. Mike based his choice on a combination of his assessment of Sammy's needs and his sense of his own strengths. He concluded that what Sammy needed most was responsibility, and so Mike, who was the youngest and least "promising" of three children in his family, decided to become big brother to Sammy who had four older sisters and no brother.

Meanwhile Thelma, another tutor in the program, was deciding on a completely different approach to take with Alvin, her tutee. She had discovered that Alvin was already responsible but very shy, so she decided to try to bring him out by making up a lot of fun word games. This points up another unique element of Youth Tutoring Youth—tutors are encouraged to create or select their own teaching materials. This helps to ensure that the tutor will be familiar with the materials and at ease with them, as Mike was with his model car. When one's instructional tools are satisfying in themselves, tutors are often pleasantly surprised at their own inventiveness.

Here are some examples of tutor-created materials:

☐ A sturdy *paper tree*, its branches hung with word cards spelling out the things seen during a walk in the park (a bug, a bird). New word cards are substituted as the vocabulary builds.

☐ *Picture analysis books*, made from magazine pictures. One tutor wrote a description of how the books were used:

Picture analysis is a game of thought where a person holds a picture with no writing in front of another person and that person is supposed to tell what the picture is saying.

In preparing their own learning materials tutors are encouraged to base them on their tutees' experience and to use the tutee himself as the starting point for instruction. This further personalizes the learning, making it more meaningful and immediate to the tutee.

I am up in the airplane. I am flying over the ocean. I am Dreaming about Being a pilot. Then I woke up and something was wrong with the airplane, so everyone put on a parachute and jumped out. David Mason

Once upon a time there were three 🐻s. They went for a 🚶 in the 🌳🌳🌳. A little came 🏃ing to their 🏠 She jumped into the baby 🛏's bed.

Dawn Kidd
Consonant Book

LONNIE

Happiness is . . .
by Richard Patterson

Some of the "texts" created by tutors and tutees.   BRUCE DOLLAR

All this emphasis on the tutors' responsibility for making their own choices may lead one to assume that the supervisor's role is relatively unimportant. On the contrary, the supervisor plays a pivotal role in determining the program's chances for success. The responsibilities of supervisors are basically threefold:

1. They must see to it that the tutors understand their responsibilities and are equipped to carry them out. This means providing effective training; it also means making tutors aware of available choices when the time comes to make a decision.

2. Supervisors must act as continuing resource persons, keeping themselves informed about methods and materials that might be useful to tutors and being available to assist tutors to make choices if such help is requested.

3. The supervisory role has been described in the *Supervisor's Manual*, which is paraphrased here:

The most critical part of the supervisor's job is hard to pin down —harder than either training the tutors or being able to help them when needed, although it is related to both. It is concerned with *granting*, really granting, responsibility to the tutors. This is a delicate process. For one thing, it is understandably difficult for any person who is officially responsible and accountable for a program to permit individuals who have neither of these responsibilities to make judgments and take action that will affect the program's success. For another thing, it is often difficult to persuade students, many of whom have long been accustomed to being told what to do, that *they* are *really* in charge of what to do. In order to be convinced, they must sense the trust and sincerity of the supervisor. And the trust and sincerity of the supervisor must be absolutely genuine; the young will not be fooled.

To a large extent, therefore, it is the supervisor's commitment to the principles outlined above that will determine the result of a program. It is a demanding but potentially highly rewarding job, as many past and current supervisors can attest. Mike's supervisor, who was supportive when called upon but also knew when to leave him alone, was very gratified to learn what Mike had said when someone asked him what he liked most about tutoring:

I get to tell other people about him (Sammy), like my mother, my girl friend, my friends. I'm learning too. I'm learning that I missed out on a lot when I was in his grade. Like consonant blends, vowels, prepositions—all those things I should've learned in the little grades when I was messing around. It helps me read better now, and it's increased my vocabulary, too.

The National Commission on Resources for Youth has identified five general conditions that it believes should characterize all YTY programs:

1. *A climate of acceptance.* This climate should exist among all school personnel, from superintendent to custodian and among the parents as well; all should be brought into the program from the very beginning, by pep talks, on-site visits, and the like.

2. *Administration.* Every program should have a competent administrator, but the truly key persons are the supervisors who meet with the tutors on a day-to-day basis. The supervisors must have real faith that the children can learn by informal methods.

3. *Space.* The program can operate in a wide variety of settings, but it is important that the tutor have a place he can call his own where he can stash his material and conduct his tutorial sessions with a reasonable degree of privacy. The tutees' elementary school is a preferred site because it helps keep the tutees' teachers in touch with and sympathetic towards the program.

4. *Tutoring sessions that are informal.* Sessions must be kept informal and must be quickly responsive to a tutee's changing needs—and sometimes even to his changing moods.

5. *Materials.* Paper, pencils, scissors, and the like are usu-

ally easy to come by, but, in addition, care must be taken to make sure that the tutor has a wide range of materials at hand —a range sufficient to meet many different kinds of learning situations and to provide opportunities for creative, often nontraditional activities.

If these five requisites are present, the National Commission has confidence that a given local program can be successful.

It is the National Commission's hope that YTY will ease its way more and more into the regular school day and that its methods of instruction will eventually have a significant leavening effect on the operations of the traditional American classroom. Some beginnings have been made, and many other programs in existence are aiming at the same objectives. The Commission realizes that the chances for success in this endeavor depend very much on convincing administrators, teachers, and parents that the instructional methods of YTY and similar programs are not merely fun and games for the children involved but are, at the same time, profound stimuli to their sometimes deep-buried desire to learn.

OTHER PROGRAMS

By the late 1960s a number of schools and related institutions were ready to accept students in a variety of teaching roles.

☐ Some of these roles grew out of the needs of black communities. For example, groups of ninth- and eleventh-grade students in White Plains, New York, received extensive instruction in African and Asian topics so that they would be able to serve as resource personnel for the city's schools— elementary, junior high, and senior high school. Some of their activities included delivering lectures and conducting seminars.

☐ In Louisville, Kentucky, twenty-eight black males, who were high school seniors, volunteered to serve as teaching assistants in local elementary schools and Head Start programs so that younger boys from fatherless homes would have daily exposure to suitable male models. The teaching assistants, who were trained in special seminars in social psychology, helped with both academic tasks and socialization tasks. They led word recognition drills, for example; they also provided encouragement and discipline, giving long hours of personal attention to the young boys.

☐ The needs of other minority groups have led to the development of different kinds of roles for young people. For example, the number of Chinese immigrants in New York City has increased sharply since the liberalization of the immigration laws in 1965, and the process of assimilating these newcomers has severely strained Chinatown's traditional social fabric. High school students, working through the Chinese Youth Council, have conducted crash courses in "Survival English" for many newly immigrated Chinese children.

☐ Some programs were designed to combat poverty and underachievement on a more general level. Jefferson High School, for example, located in a poor section of Portland, Oregon, organized a vast program called Student Tutor and Assistant Teacher Program (STAT). As many as two hundred high school students, working under the supervision of senior high and elementary school teachers, were employed during the school day as classroom tutors.

☐ The character of still other programs was determined by the curriculum demands rather than by socio-economic considerations. In the Cherry Creek schools near Denver, Colorado, high school students were recruited to aid elementary school teachers teach science. Teams of five or six high school students, matched with groups of five or six elementary school students, worked in elementary school classrooms for three hours a week.

☐ In the Ontario-Montclair School District in southern California, tutoring in math and reading is an elective course for junior high school students. One day each week these students work in a one-to-one relationship with fourth-, fifth-, and sixth-graders from nearby elementary schools. On another day each week the tutors get together to discuss problems they have encountered with their tutees and to devise possible solutions. This project was funded under Title III, ESEA.

☐ Another southern California school that has an extensive tutoring program is the elementary school in Pacoima, which is near Los Angeles. For children in grades K through two, the major source of reading instruction is not the adult teacher but a tutor from a more advanced grade. Tutoring pervades the school. It is used not only with older children teaching younger children but also within classes—especially in grades four, five, and six. Children teach each other reading, math, and other school subjects. All of the fifteen hundred children in the school are involved in tutoring—either tutoring, being tutored, or both. Also, as in the Ontario-Montclair School District, students from the nearby junior high school tutor children in the elementary school.

☐ In North Wildwood, New Jersey, the Technical Recreation Center provided not only the more traditional basketball hoops and pool tables but also rooms full of electronic "junk." Out of this material, students of all ages learned from each other—younger from older, but often enough, older from younger, too—and created real working devices: buzzers, flashlights, radios, or whatever the materials at hand suggested.

A FURTHER WORD

Many of these programs are still in operation; several have expanded, and untold numbers of similar projects have sprung up in all sections of the country. This is genuinely encouraging, because there are few ideas in education today that are more dynamic. The next decade should see still further exploration of the educational values of children teaching children.

YOUTH
as community
manpower

Here, under our long hair, our grubby clothes, and our free ways, you can see that we have in our hearts a compassion and a need to help.

I like the way the kids feel toward me when I come in each day. It's important to them to see one of us around. You can see this in lots of ways. For weeks I worked really hard with one boy. Then, one day, he put his hand out to me and shook mine. That as one of the most important things that happened to me. Suddenly he recognized me. These children are wonderful.

The United States has many agencies and institutions that have been created to provide important public services. They include mental hospitals, old age homes, museums, day care centers, public transportation, health and sanitation facilities; they include such service people as firemen, policemen, and welfare workers. Money and dedication are required to keep these service institutions functioning effectively. If funds are cut back for any reason, or if funds are not increased as public needs increase, there is an inevitable gap between services needed and services available. Such a gap exists today; funds to provide the needed resources—including the vital ingredient of an adequate number of competent, dedicated people— are simply not keeping pace with public needs.

This service gap creates an important challenge to the United States to use its human resources in new ways. At the national level, VISTA and the Teachers Corps are two examples of responses to this challenge. On the local level, programs for developing the potentialities of volunteer manpower have proliferated, and, increasingly, these programs are focusing on what is probably the largest, the most zestful, and the most underused manpower pool of all—the nation's youth.

These young people have great potential. For one thing they mature earlier than they used to. Television and the other mass media have helped to give them a keener and more sophisticated perception of the world around them than the young people growing up before 1950 had at a comparable age. At the same time, these young people are expected to spend an ever increasing number of years in school where they are usually allowed to make only theoretical applications of their perceptions about themselves and their world. Fortunately, however, they are both eager to break out of their isolation and increasingly capable of doing so effectively. One evidence of this breakthrough is the growing number of programs that permit and encourage high school students to contribute their manpower to community public service.

The school's role in these programs is of fundamental importance, because if public service jobs are to be performed effectively and if the person doing them is to derive proper satisfaction, training is crucial. Schools can make the manpower contributions of high school students invaluable by providing training programs for those who would like to work in a community service program, and by integrating the students' community service with an overall educational program.

The possibilities open to high school students who would like to contribute manpower to their communities are almost limitless and so are the possibilities open to schools. The programs described in this chapter represent only a small sampling of these opportunities.

HIGH SCHOOL ARCHEOLOGY PROJECTS
GEORGIA

Archeology is generally not considered to be a vital part of today's life. It will not feed the earth's hungry nor put an end to war and strife. But some of the lessons from the past could be vital to our culture's survival in the future. At the Pebblebrook High School [Cobb County, Georgia] site . . . man occupied the land for some 6,000 years. For 5,000 years of that time, he drew his entire subsistence from the surrounding natural resources without disrupting the balance of nature to the point he was forced off the soil. The white man has resided in the area for less than one hundred forty years, and already the water and air are polluted to the point of breaking the ecological chain upon which man depends to sustain life.[1]

1. Lawrence Meier, Edward I. Dittmar, and Glen C. Williams. "An Appraisal of the Archeological Resources, Cobb and Fulton Counties, Georgia, and Other Related Areas of the Chattahoochee River Valley," July 1971, unpublished.

This statement from an archeologist who was involved points up the seldom recognized relationship between archeology and the survival of our culture. Students engaged in the archeological projects in Georgia have discovered this relationship for themselves.

Cobb County

Cobb County, located next door to Atlanta, Georgia, has recently been experiencing rapid population growth and rapid commercial development. It is also an area that was heavily settled during different periods of the prehistory era. In 1968, 1969, and 1970, archeologists working under the direction of an emeritus professor of the University of Georgia discovered and excavated an entire large village that flourished two thousand years ago. The report of this achievement made its way into the national press and into the *National Geographic*'s "Man's Past in the Americas." But the dream of local Georgian archeologists to come to understand the nature of life in prehistoric Cobb County has been seriously threatened by the rapid pace of human and commercial expansion in their area. In the words of one member of the Cobb County archeological survey:

A brief glance at the materials collected during the past three years' work shows that by conservative estimates the area traversed by the Chattahoochee River from Buford Dam to the line of south Fulton County has been occupied by man for at least ten thousand years. During some periods of prehistory the valley was heavily settled and this is again true today. However, the present settlement is expanding so rapidly and changing the face of the land so drastically that it will destroy all traces of the former inhabitants.[2]

One of the volunteer excavators at the site of the two-

2. Ibid.

thousand-year-old village was a student at Pebblebrook High School. When he returned to school, he noticed that his own schoolyard seemed to offer up pieces of pottery and other artifacts that were remarkably similar to those found at the village. Archeologists who worked on the village project took time to inspect the school grounds and discovered, to the considerable surprise of the community, that a twenty-two-acre plot of land outside the school building was laced with prehistoric materials of archeological significance. They also learned that a new six-foot pipeline was about to be laid right through the middle of the site. This is a classic example of the kind of emergency that archeologists face all over the country. In this situation the archeologists knew that the evidences of ancient human life locked in the soil of Pebblebrook High School would be destroyed forever unless a salvage operation could be mounted immediately.

It then occurred to the members of the archeological group that a financially feasible way of organizing an emergency salvage operation at Pebblebrook High School would be to use the students as labor. Voluntary labor on archeology digs has generally been done by people who are of college age or older, and often this volunteer manpower is not available in sufficient quantity or at the right time. In this case the pipeline's construction schedule forced the archeologists to ask for help from the students in the high school.

They went first to the principal to enlist his help in working out a proposal to submit to the Cobb County Board of Education. The proposal, based on the belief that high school students *could* perform the tedious, time-consuming, and difficult work required to salvage the site, was presented to the Board and was accepted. The Board agreed to sponsor at Pebblebrook a program that was strikingly novel and significant in its implications.

From the fifty students who applied for the program, only those who had two study hall periods a day were selected.

For a period of four weeks, these sixteen students devoted half of their school day to salvage work on Pebblebrook's prehistoric site. The archeologists who had conceived the idea and a graduate student in anthropology from the University of Georgia supervised the on-site work; a history teacher from the school served as the project's liaison with the school system. The Cobb County Board of Education agreed to allocate a small amount of money for the project's expenses with the understanding that a comparable sum would be raised by community groups. Work was begun on March 9, 1970; the bulldozers were to begin construction on the pipeline in four weeks.

Almost immediately it was apparent that high school students were competent at archeological work. Each student was assigned to one archeological feature at a time and was responsible for excavating that feature and keeping field notes on his work. The students were both enthusiastic and careful. They asked pertinent questions and never complained, even when given the most tedious tasks. According to the archeologists who had initiated the idea of using high school students, the young people were more able than most older people to evaluate their discoveries because they were less easily shocked by the differences between contemporary civilization and the culture they were uncovering. They responded eagerly to the related studies that were introduced to them. Lectures and slide shows were presented on such subjects as cultural geography, environmental ecology, primitive economics, and subsistence and cultural patterns; a geologist was called in to interpret certain geological formations; an agronomist and an ethno-botanist came in to sample and analyze various soils.

As time for the pipeline's construction drew near, the dedication of the students increased. They began putting in many extra hours, even though they were receiving no academic credit or pay and had to make up all missed school assignments. At the close of the four-week period, twenty archeo-

A teacher and students digging up artifacts in their schoolyard
as bulldozers prepare the way for a pipeline.   J. C. LEE

logical features had been excavated, recorded, and analyzed in terms of chronology, cultural affiliation, and extent of occupation.

Questionnaires were distributed to all the student participants and to all their teachers. Student comments included: "I have learned to be more observant and more interesting [sic]" and "I have learned to make better use of my time. It helped me develop into a more responsible person." Teachers reported improvement in grades, attention spans, and attitudes, with the most substantial improvement taking place among those who had been regarded as the poorest students. The program's success was so obvious that the school board agreed to continue it on an expanded basis through the remaining twelve weeks of the school year. The bulldozers were on the site too, but students worked around them, and the bulldozers obligingly worked around the students.

At the county level, the government authorized a county-wide summer archeology program for high school students to survey all the right-of-ways for new county pipelines. This was in response to the archeologists' assertion that, since the pipelines followed all the major streams, they would destroy nearly all of the prehistoric human remains in both Fulton and Cobb counties.

The success of these early programs led to the establishment of a temporary archeology program in several Cobb County schools, including Pebblebrook where the bulk of the archeological activity took place. While the program was in existence, some thirty students participated in field projects during the first and third of the school's three terms. After a one-week orientation period built around slide presentations of the program's operations during the previous terms, three emergency sites facing impending destruction were researched.

To participate in the program, a student first applied to his counselor. He was accepted if he had passing grades and two scheduled study halls, and if the program had not reached its maximum enrollment of forty students per term. (Some consideration was given to limiting enrollment to seniors, so that participants would be able to follow up their experience immediately with college work.)

Students worked for two hours every day during the nine-week term. A major development was that participants received one and one-half term credits on a pass/fail basis. During the winter term, an anthropology course was given by a Pebblebrook teacher who followed outlines developed by himself and the program's professional archeologists. Students who enrolled in the archeology project were not required to take the course, but many wished to do so. A student was not permitted to take more than one full year of work in archeology/anthropology.

The program at one site was rather ingeniously financed. Its supervisors were placed on the payroll of the Cobb County government; the Cobb County government, in turn, received subsidies, amounting to one-third the cost of the whole project, from the federal government under Public Law 91-660. This law provided money, through the Environmental Protection Agency, for local efforts aimed at combatting environmental damage caused by federally-funded projects such as the new sewage system in Cobb County. The chief expenses of the archeological program were the part-time salaries of its three supervisors and its two graduate student helpers.

One hundred and forty-two students participated directly in the archeology program at Pebblebrook; almost a thousand other students had some exposure to the school's archeology site through lectures, graphic presentations, and other means. The program was considered a rich and many-faceted learning experience. Teachers in all subject areas noticed great improvements in the morale and academic performance of student participants. Within the program itself the archeologists observed growth in all the important intellectual traits that mark successful archeological work: patience, careful elaboration of argument, sensitivity to detail, and adherence to logic combined with respect for intuition.

This intellectual growth accompanied personality growth. The students usually worked in teams of two to four persons, and a spirit of shared inquiry that developed within the teams made the project practically self-policing. If one student did lazy or faulty work, the others were quick to insist that he do better, and for the sake of the group, he did do better. Moreover, the salvaging work was different enough from everyday school work so that the enthusiasm and the skills of those who had been regarded as the "poorest" students made them the equals of the "best" students. This had a substantial democratizing effect on students, breaking down a number of questionable and potentially damaging distinctions between "A" students and "D" students. At least two other dynamic ideas were vividly impressed on these young people. The first was the idea that hard physical work—digging, sweating, bending over, sorting little bits of unknown things—can be intimately related to intellectual endeavor. The second was the human identity that came with the discovery of a personal relationship to the vast and complex history of the life of man.

Atlanta

The Cobb County archeology program stirred up great interest in Atlanta, located in neighboring Fulton County. As a result of that interest, the Atlanta Public Schools now include archeology as one of the components of its Exploration Quarter, an innovative program inaugurated in 1968.

The Exploration Quarter provides an opportunity for high school students to do in-depth study in an area that is of great interest to them but is not included in the regular curriculum. The Atlanta schools have four quarters per year, and participation in the Exploration Quarter program is limited to thirty students per quarter.

Students apply for admission to the program; those who are accepted may spend as much as two academic quarters studying and working on assignments of their own choosing. A coordinator meets with students to help them develop and evaluate their projects and their progress, and high school credit is given in accordance with established criteria.

Archeology has become one of the main interest areas in the Exploratory Quarter with ten students participating in the fall of 1972 and more participating in 1973. Students who choose archeology as their interest area spend full time working in the field and in the special laboratory that has been provided for them.

Geology, cultural geography, botany, and cultural anthropology are encountered right on the site. In addition to the natural and the social sciences, students become involved with mathematics and engineering because of their bearing on their work. For example, students must use sophisticated mathematical operations to calculate the total size of a piece of pottery from the fragments they find in the field. Engineering is needed to map the topography of a site.

In the laboratory the Atlanta Public Schools set up in one of the school buildings, students carry out the various phases of artifact analysis, photography of specimens, drafting of site plans, and preparation of reports.

One of the most interesting and challenging elements of the archeological projects is their potential for being replicated in practically any part of the nation. Not every school, of course, has a prehistory site right on its own grounds, but many communities contain potential digs, and more of these will be discovered as interest develops. In New York City, for example, in the Bedford-Stuyvesant community, young people have uncovered evidences of a rather well-to-do black settlement which was there in the late nineteenth century. Prior to this discovery, it had been assumed that the area had always been inhabited by impoverished blacks.

It is important to recognize that many potential digs are minor and are repetitive in terms of the information they would yield. Since not all sites can be excavated, there is legitimate debate about how much of our resources we must be willing to commit to archeology. The availability of high school manpower needs to be taken into account in making decisions on these points, particularly with reference to resources needed.

The young people who have become involved in archeology in the two projects described have exhibited competence, patience, self-confidence, and modesty that are characteristics of effective archeologists. Already they have made a real contribution to their culture. And whether that contribution is recognized now or at some future time, the students themselves believe in the value of archeological work and derive satisfaction from doing something they recognize as significant for society and for their own learning and living.

Finally, the Cobb County and Atlanta projects strongly suggest that there are a number of ways in which archeology can become an effective, integral part of a school program, challenging students to learn through activities that are both action and academically oriented.

SCHOOL AND COMMUNITY SERVICE PROJECT
RAMAPO, NEW YORK

The School and Community Service Project developed by the Ramapo Central School District No. 2 in Spring Valley, New York, differs from the Cobb County archeology project in at least one fundamental respect: in Cobb County, a community problem was the prime motive for establishing a school service program; in Ramapo, a student problem was the prime motive.

Rockland County, where the Ramapo district is located, is primarily a "bedroom community" for the city of New York.

Its young people feel out of touch with their parents, with real work, and with the diversity of resources available to young people in the community. Ramapo students have tended to lack self-esteem, and many have turned to drugs. Ramapo's superintendent of schools thought that students' alienation from their community might begin to disappear and their self-esteem might begin to increase, if young people had opportunities to work for community service organizations. At the same time, the Ramapo Central School District No. 2 was well aware of the need to design a community service program based on a genuine community problem, not on an artificial or contrived need. The project coordinator searched for community needs that Ramapo students could respond to with competence and with confidence that their help was valuable. He developed a long list of needs and opportunities —and Ramapo students are now busy. The following activities are only a few of the community services that are being provided by students; there are many others:

☐ Mental Health Complex in Pomona—Students play games with patients, organize activities, and read and tell stories.

☐ New York Rehabilitation Hospital in Haverstraw—Students help with physical therapy.

☐ West Street Day Care Center in Spring Valley—Students work with children ages three to five.

☐ Rockland County Infirmary in Pomona—Students write letters for patients, take them for walks, and lead discussion groups.

☐ Camp Jawonio in New City—Students assist in developing physical skills in the physically handicapped through therapy and games.

☐ Boy Scouts in New City—Students help organize new troops and assist with their camping programs.

Ramapo's School and Community Service Project is not a complicated program. Any student at either of the District's two high schools, Spring Valley or Ramapo, who chooses to participate, who spends forty hours working with a community service organization, and who has a reasonable attendance at the program's seminars receives school credit equivalent to a one-semester course. For one hundred hours of activity which includes community service work plus attendance at seminars and at counseling sessions with advisors, a student receives credit equal to a full-year course. The hours do not have to be accumulated within any given semester but must be completed within a given school year.

The program now has almost seven hundred student participants ranging in age from fourteen through eighteen. Within the total student population of three thousand four hundred and fifty, there are some students who still know little about the program or are skeptical about it. Special efforts are made to inform them about the activities, rouse their interest, and encourage them to become involved.

Any student who wishes to participate simply signs up and selects a service area from among those identified by the coordinator. If a student is not able, for one reason or another, to work in the area he has chosen, it is sometimes possible for him to change to another area. But changes are made only after discussion between the advisor and student and after a full review of the situation. Reasons for the requested change are considered carefully, and the new assignment possibilities are explored thoroughly before a change is implemented. Dropouts from the program are few in number, and this reflects the efforts of advisors to counsel students and provide the kind of support needed to help the young people achieve success and satisfaction from their service activities.

The coordinator of the School and Community Service Project is assisted by two other full-time professional staff members—a School and Community Service advisor in each of the two participating high schools. The budget for the program comes entirely from District funds, and the money is used almost exclusively for salaries and mandatory fringe benefits for its three staff personnel.

Initially, students were not involved in planning and implementing the Community Service Project, but that situation has changed. Since the spring of 1972, there has been a School and Community Service Program Advisory Committee made up of students, classroom teachers, parents, agency officials, and program staff members. This Committee, representing all the groups involved and advisory in nature, meets to review the total operation, to examine the current status of the program, and to suggest improvements.

Individual students may develop and implement their own programs. And groups of students sharing a common interest often work together to develop, organize, and plan how to implement programs that they then operate at a particular school or agency.

A number of techniques for evaluating the effectiveness of the School and Community Service Project are now in use with the major focus on student growth and development. For example, a student self-evaluation questionnaire was developed by three staff members with assistance from the Director of Pupil Personnel Services and the involvement of students themselves. When a student begins his service project, he fills out the questionnaire and places it, unsigned, in a sealed envelope. After he completes his service program, he again fills out the questionnaire. At this point, he opens the envelope containing his questionnaire and compares his responses on the two forms. This provides him an opportunity to observe his growth and development.

A second evaluative technique is a quantitative measurement device that is completed by the student's on-the-job supervisor at the end of each semester. This provides a judgment of student personal growth from the point of view of the supervising adult.

The logs students keep are still another resource for evaluation. So too are the observations of the advisors in group seminar settings and in individual counseling sessions.

Various evaluation techniques will be reviewed and revised as changes appear to be desirable.

In the early days of its existence, the School and Community Service Project had a serious transportation problem. Suburban Rockland County has practically no public transportation, and only a relatively small number of students have cars. Since it was difficult for many students to work at sites located great distances from their schools, many young people worked in school-related jobs simply because they were easy to get to, and many others just didn't become involved in the program. In the 1972–73 school budget, however, funds for transportation were allocated to the project so there is now money to operate mini-buses where necessary. This has made it possible for more students without cars to become involved in activities in agencies some distance from school.

If this and other funding continues, and more and more students become effectively involved in the School and Community Service Project, then there is probably greater likelihood that the project will become completely integrated with the school program.

Attitudes of many participants toward their local community seem to have improved perceptibly: students feel more a part of the community than they ever did before; drug abuse among participants seems to have declined markedly; and there are many evidences of various kinds of personal growth and development. For example, a boy who signed up to work at a mental hospital heard that during the previous year a patient had been violently attacked by a group of other patients. He went to his job filled with fear but eventually discovered that the people he was there to help were as afraid of him as he was of them. With work and involvement, his fears subsided. Another boy, who had the evangelical commitment to Jesus that has recently begun to appear among the nation's youth, has spent his service time working in a church with some of the most notorious young hoodlums and drug addicts in Rockland County. He has helped some thirty of these young people.

The program's effect on the adult community has been equally encouraging. Community support is reflected in the letters of praise that are constantly being sent to the Board of Education and in the radio shows and newspaper editorials that give frequent and favorable publicity to the Project.

In a later development at Ramapo, thirty students now serve as apprentices or interns for individuals who operate locate businesses or who are engaged in a profession. These include photographers, chefs, mechanics, lawyers, doctors, and veterinarians. The students choose from the names of professionals who have offered to work with a student. The equivalent of one full-course credit is given to students who spend forty hours in a semester with one of the professionals. So far most students have spent far more than forty hours, and few want to leave their job when the semester is over.

DUO (Do Unto Others)
VERMONT

In Vermont's DUO project, as in Ramapo's School and Community Service Program, the students' welfare was the prime *raison d'être*. The Vermont situation was slightly different from Ramapo insofar as the student alienation sensed by Ramapo administrators did not seem to be so acute nor so widespread in Vermont. Nevertheless, there was an underlying current of student anxiety, and this was the reason why DUO came into existence.

DUO differs from Ramapo's Community Service Program in at least two noteworthy respects. The first is the range of freedom it offers to participants; the second is the point of origin. DUO originated within the Vermont State Board of Education and was introduced into schools on a state-wide basis.

The way DUO was brought to the Vermont schools is a good example of how change can be effectively initiated. DUO grew out of discussions between Vermont's Commissioner of Education and a one-year intern in the Vermont Department of Education. Their discussions were stimulated by a letter to the editor that recommended a national civilian service program as an alternative to the military draft. The Commissioner and the intern discussed community needs for manpower, the ways in which students could help meet those needs, and the desire of students for more action-oriented education.

When this community service project was established, it had four basic guidelines. Later these guidelines were modified somewhat to provide still further flexibility in the program. These modifications are noted parenthetically, immediately following the statement of the original guideline.

1. A DUO project should last for one-half of an academic year, and a full semester of academic credit should be granted to the student for his work in the community.

2. The student's community work must be full time and must last for a semester. (*A later change now allows for partial credit for partial service. A student, for example, may work anywhere from one day a week to full time during his service work semester.*)

3. The student must take the initiative by selecting a particular service agency and identifying the work he could do that would fit into the agency's program. (*Some exceptions to this guideline have been made. Occasionally, for example, a school coordinator may compile a list of organizations that have used DUO's service in the past and make it available to a student who seems to need help in getting ideas for his project.*)

4. The school must monitor the student's performance. This is done through counseling sessions and periodic seminars called Forums. The Forums are organized by review boards made up of teachers, students, and members of the community; the methods of selecting persons to serve on a review board vary from school to school.

The high level support of the Commissioner helped to win quick approval for DUO from the State Board of Education. DUO was conceived early in the summer of 1969; by August it was official state policy to permit Vermont schools to grant a full semester's credit for students participating in a program that conformed to DUO's four guidelines.

The next step for the Department of Education's young interns was to sell the idea to Vermont's schools and develop local interest. From the very beginning it was recognized that only those schools that developed enthusiasm for the idea and decided to become involved with DUO without pressure from the State Board would be truly good prospects. By deliberate choice, therefore, the state offered schools no money incentives of any kind for establishing DUO and provided no specifics on how the program was to operate aside from the four guidelines just mentioned. The intern went around the state explaining these four guidelines to local people, assuring them that the State Board had a long-term commitment to DUO, and showing them the many letters he had collected from colleges and universities all over the country stating that participation in DUO would *not* jeopardize a student's chances for admission.

The intern's job was to convince Vermont's schools that their effectiveness in fulfilling their educational responsibilities would not be threatened by making "school" something larger than the school building, something that can take students out into the community and leave them there for long periods of learning. On the contrary, their effectiveness might well be increased. The intern was very successful. He talked about ideas rather than about detailed programs, and he imposed nothing that would stifle local imagination. He found that the superintendent in each school district was nearly always the key person; if he could be convinced, DUO would be accepted. Before the DUO idea was a year old, one-fourth of Vermont's high schools had some form of DUO program. Today a third of Vermont's high schools are enrolled in DUO, and some sixteen hundred students have participated in a service project.

There is still no state financial help for DUO programs, there is no state office assigned to watch over DUO or collect information about it, and there has never been a state evaluation of DUO's success. It is not Vermont's way to bury a good idea with bureaucracy—and perhaps this is something other state departments of education should bear in mind as they approach the problem of introducing change into their schools.

Perhaps the best way to get an idea of how DUO operates is to look fairly closely at a local program in operation. Of the state's three largest DUO programs, one is run by Mount Saint Joseph High School, a Catholic school in Rutland; the other two are in public schools—Bennington's Mt. Anthony Union High School, and Champlain Valley Union High School. The operational pattern at Mount Saint Joseph High School is representative of many DUO programs and is described here.

The DUO coordinator at Mount Saint Joseph is a faculty member who carries a full teaching load in addition to DUO. She puts in very long hours and hopes that she will soon be released from some of her classroom duties. Any student interested in DUO must first see her for help in preparing a proposal to be submitted to the Review Board for approval. The proposal can be brief, but it must answer the following questions:

What is the proposed project?
What are the student's goals?

How will the project benefit the community?

How will it benefit the student?

Where and with whom will the student be working?

What specifically will the student be doing?

What preliminary planning and information will the student need to prepare himself for the project?

How will the student know if he is succeeding in his goals?

How will the student share his experience with others at the school?

In its original design, DUO sought to require an extremely high degree of self-motivation: the student would have to find a project entirely by himself and make sure that the particular community organization he wanted to work for would accept him. At Mount Saint Joseph, however, the coordinator now helps perhaps half of DUO's applicants meet these requirements. She has a list of local organizations that have accepted DUO students in the past, and she makes information from that list available to students who want to work on a DUO project but haven't been able to find anything suitable on their own.

After he prepares his proposal, the student's next step is to appear before the DUO Review Board. The Review Board at Mount Saint Joseph consists of fourteen people, including faculty members, the school's principal, former DUO students, community service agency personnel, and other community members. The Board considers the feasibility of a student's proposal, and if a majority of the members approve it, a contract is established between the Board and the student. The contract commits the student to work on his DUO project for a full semester in exchange for a semester of school credit. At Mount Saint Joseph, sixty proposals were approved for one particular semester.

The DUO participants come from a range of classes and achievement levels, and participants are almost equally divided between male and female. Some students plan to work as a group and others as individuals, but each participant is affiliated with some community service agency. Mount Saint Joseph supports the idea of students working *independently* rather than with an agency, but so far no such projects have been fully developed. Perhaps sometime soon Mount Saint Joseph students will be working on independent DUO projects along with a number of other Vermont schools that already have independent projects.

During his DUO semester, a student is required to work full time on his project; at the minimum, he should put in as many hours as he would have spent in school. He is also required to appear periodically at Forums sponsored by the school's Review Board, where small groups of DUO students discuss the problems they have encountered and the progress they have made. At the end of the semester, the student must once again appear before the Review Board. Both the student and the Review Board are required to make a final evaluation of the student's performance. It has been the practice at Mount Saint Joseph to award credit to a student even if he did a poor job, but the Review Board's evaluation of low quality performance is then attached to the student's transcript.

The DUO program at Mount Saint Joseph continues to operate without any special budget allocation whatever. If the program coordinator is released from some of her classroom load, then it would have to be said that at least some resources were going to DUO, but even a partial salary would represent only a very modest allocation for such a worthwhile program. Some outside consultants doubt DUO's capacity to survive long without some kind of permanent budgetary allowance. They feel that once the program's initial excitement wears off, faculty members will be less willing to volunteer large blocks of time to the program, and money will be needed to keep it going. Mount Saint Joseph does not think this will happen at its school.

DUO's success is widely recognized in Vermont. DUO students can point to a wide variety of new learning dimensions that the program has opened for them: development of confidence in their ability to start and organize a practical project; sound advice on careers; awareness of such realities as that poverty exists in the communities where they live; and an awareness of the individuality of people they had previously generalized about.

The response of local communities has been heart-warming. At Mount Saint Joseph, for example, the program coordinator spends a part of each day answering requests from local service groups for student assistance. Such cooperation from the local community is encouraging.

Perhaps the greatest single obstacle that DUO programs have faced is the parental opposition that historically surfaces when a new program is introduced. The parents' worries are understandable; permitting children to be out of the school building for a whole semester is a radical departure from traditional education. Parents often fear that their children will learn nothing, sometimes think that the school is abdicating its responsibilities, and worry that their child's chances of getting into the "right" college and career will be jeopardized. Numerous orientation meetings for parents of the program's first participants did, in most cases, alleviate such concerns. Parental permission is required for participation in any of the state's DUO programs, and in most cases parents give consent. Once the program had been tried at a school, parents can see the success of the preceding class of DUO participants, and opposition declines markedly.

Another problem, academic in nature, stems from the fact that participation in DUO means a whole semester away from school. Students taking sequential subjects must break up their sequences, and in mathematics, foreign languages, music, art, or any advanced special training, this may have some adverse effect on a student's progress. Concern about this has led many college bound students in Rutland to wait until the second semester of their senior year before getting involved in DUO. The coordinators, however, feel it is desirable for students to participate during the sophomore or junior year. One solution is to allow students who are seriously pursuing a particular field to take a school course while they work with DUO projects. Some DUO participants have, in fact, kept up from a third to a half day of classes.

Out of the many experiences of DUO programs in all parts of Vermont, certain bits of advice can be extracted for those who might consider starting comparable programs elsewhere. The first bit of advice is that sympathetic personnel should be placed in all the program's administrative positions. Students seem to depend on their coordinators and Review Boards in more complex and often more personal ways than they depend on regular teachers.

Second, Review Boards must examine the proposals of students very carefully, and insist—firmly but also with sensitivity—that, before beginning work on any project, a student have a clear and precise idea of what his project requires and what he hopes to accomplish. In the early stages of a DUO project is it easy for a student to set goals that will overwhelm him later. A Review Board, through the Forum mechanism, should diligently search out any students who are having difficulties with their projects and help them back on the right path. The Forums are an extremely important mechanism for preventing panic, frustration, and failure.

The third bit of advice comes from Mount Saint Joseph's coordinator. She says that in addition to being diligent, the Review Board and coordinator must also be extremely generous in assessing the motives of students who apply to DUO. They must not be quick to conclude, for example, that a student who presents an inadequately prepared proposal is just trying to escape a semester of schoolwork. In her experience, students rarely use DUO this way, and she feels that an inadequate proposal more often reflects problems that the coordinator or Review Board can help the student to solve.

Finally, there is advice from a student who worked as a member of a conservation group. The advice was not directed toward administrators, but it may offer them true insight into the nature of the program and of education itself:

> Don't believe everything you read about it. . . . Yes, it was worthwhile. I got to see spring for the first time in years—it's so basic it's like an abstract idea . . . it was not in terms of production, technological solutions—it was a human experience for me . . . it was alive for me. You have to do it under your own steam. You pass or fail in your own eyes—it's you who you have to answer to. It makes you self-aware. I think for a lot of kids it wasn't just being out of school . . . once you become responsible . . . you realize your potential isn't as important as what you DO produce. It's a real experience. It's a reality. School is not real.

OTHER PROGRAMS

Many programs besides those just described provide opportunities for young people to contribute manpower for various kinds of needed community services, and many other programs such as the following are developing.

□ The School-Community Service Project of the San Mateo, California, Union School District, for instance, is especially interesting because of the way it involves students in many of the community's most basic and essential public services. Some San Mateo students contribute their labor to the police department, organizing and carrying out repair schedules for the Department's cars. Others are trained by the fire department in all the basic fire-fighting tasks—use of tools and equipment, care and use of fire hose, salvage work, first aid, and rescue operations. They then become auxiliary firemen, on call in case of emergency.

The entire program now includes thirteen hundred students in a wide variety of community jobs. These students are eligible to receive five school credits per semester for eighty-five hours of volunteer work and are permitted to do their volunteer work during one or two hours of each school day.

☐ The High School Volunteer Services program in New Haven, Connecticut, is particularly interesting because of the unusual degree to which students have control over the program. High School Volunteer Services is basically a placement office for all New Haven students who would like to do volunteer community work. There is one adult consultant, but all of the program's administrative positions are filled by students. Organizations that have used the office's volunteers include the American Red Cross, the Board of Education, the National Multiple Sclerosis Society, the Council of Churches, and Yale University's Peabody Museum of Natural History.

☐ The Youth Elderly Services (YES) program of Fall River, Massachusetts, shows that programs devoted to service in a single institution can be as stimulating as broader-based programs, and in some cases the sharp focus they provide can lead to experiences of exceptional intensity. In YES high school students establish one-to-one or small group relationships with elderly people in Fall River's nursing homes. High school students commit one or two hours a week to meet with their elderly friends, many of whom have no other contact with people younger than themselves. The meetings often result in deep ties, and the high school students write letters, perform errands for those who can't get around, and help with recreational activities. Perhaps the most important thing they do is simply to sit and talk with these elderly and often lonely people and help give them a feeling that young people care about them.

☐ At Sonoma State Hospital, a California institution for the mentally retarded and physically handicapped, groups of teenagers from Palo Alto arrive regularly to work mainly with

Physical therapy often leads to great affection between a young patient and a student volunteer.   BRADLEY WRIGHT

children but in some cases with older patients as well. Over the weekends, the young volunteers leave early to make the drive one hundred miles to Eldridge where the hospital is located. Many students also spend their vacation working at the Sonoma Hospital. In fact, the volunteers have taken over an old barn on the hospital grounds, remodeled it, and fashioned it into living quarters they call Volunteer Village.

These young people spend hours taking patients out for walks, assisting with physical therapy, reading to patients, playing with children, initiating arts and crafts activities, and much, much more. In this, as in other successful service programs, the teenagers receive training and support from competent and sympathetic adults. Hospital personnel provide some of the training, and students often attend night classes taught by pediatricians, psychiatrists, occupational therapists, and other professionals. With this background, the young volunteers are able to work with patients in such areas as motor coordination, water therapy, and sensory and motor stimulation. Several of the teenagers have found the experience of working with the mentally retarded and physically handicapped so rewarding that they have decided to take up professional or paraprofessional careers in these fields.

One of the most important things these young people do is provide a source of comfort, love, and companionship for the patients. A "TLC" program ("tender loving care" on a one-to-one basis) has been started to provide a small number of patients with a continuous sustained relationship. Some volunteers become so attached to their TLC patients that they often leave notes for the next group of volunteers in the hope that someone will continue with their patients.

I would very much like someone to continue working with Jody. . . . She is adorable, and I think she is greatly improved because of the attention given to her. She is very responsive and giggles when you tickle her or even hold her hand. One problem she has is holding her head up. The way to help her with this is to put her in a position where her head is dangling and sometimes she will lift it up. Take her out on the lawn and play with her. If it's not too hot out put her in the sun a few minutes, she's so pale. She blinks in the sun but she's blind so it couldn't be bad for her. Also there are some directions on the back of her bed for how she should be positioned (by the therapist). If you can figure them out please do them because the techs never do. Be good to her, she's an angel.

Love
Martha

The volunteers have developed a strong group spirit; they clearly love their project, and their love shows through to Sonoma's patients.

A FURTHER WORD

One of the important aspects of all the community manpower programs described in this chapter is their relatively low cost to the schools. Under some circumstances, money may have to be provided for administration, transportation, or special instruction, but since the major part of the students' program experience takes place outside the school walls, many classroom costs may actually be reduced.

Considering the high capabilities of young people and their eagerness to help perform the public services that all our communities need, it would seem to make simple good sense for schools to take advantage of the potential of these programs to enhance student learning as well as to provide needed community service. The schools and community groups that have undertaken student programs have been more ·than satisfied. In Cobb County, Ramapo, Vermont, San Mateo, New Haven, Fall River, and Palo Alto, the experiences have demonstrated that significant learning takes place and important services are provided when students are properly prepared and then released to contribute their manpower to community public service.

YOUTH
as entrepreneurs

I really didn't count on learning this—that I could do things that would make money for people and that I could even spend that money.

Six months ago, when I came here, I felt like a very weak person. I really didn't have a sense that I could do anything for myself out in the big world. But working here I was forced to stand on my own two feet. Well, I didn't like the work itself so much, but I really loved what we were making—and that I had some control over it—how it was to look and how much it was going to cost.

In the United States adolescents such as those quoted above have always performed substantial and varied money-earning roles. In the earlier days of our country's history, opportunities were somewhat limited in scope—working on a farm, delivering newspapers and groceries, mowing lawns, or helping with various household chores. Some of these activities continue today. Adolescent boys still deliver newspapers, messages, and groceries; but they also pump gas, wash cars, and help with repair jobs on radios, TV sets, bicycles, cars, and motorcycles. Adolescent girls baby-sit, work in neighborhood stores, or serve as receptionists in offices.

Increasingly, money-earning tasks are shared by boys and girls. This is true of such things as tutoring, working in stores, participating in storytelling or story-reading hours in local libraries, engaging in amateur theatricals, and organizing and helping with recycling projects of many kinds.

Child labor laws, which have changed drastically over the years, have played a part in the working roles of young people. Earlier in our history the absence of restrictions permitted damaging exploitation of young children. Later this situation was corrected—overcorrected in some instances; today, most child labor laws leave some avenues open for young people to earn money. In general our society attaches value to experiences and opportunities that help young people acquire work skills, develop positive attitudes about working, and provide bases for making judgments about future employment.

In spite of the positive attitudes, however, ideas about the place of entrepreneurial roles for young people continue to be contradictory and confusing. These contradictory and confusing ideas are present in the schools as well as in society generally, and they have sometimes contributed to student absenteeism and to dropping out of school. The traditional attitude is—school hours are for schoolwork; out-of-school hours are for "real" work. Schoolwork and "real" work have often clashed. Morning paperboys and late-at-night babysitters are often too tired to be alert students. Girls and boys who work after school can't play intramural sports, can't participate in writing and publishing a school newspaper, and can't engage in debating or drama activities, if such activities are regarded as extracurricular, after-school opportunities rather than integral parts of the regular school program.

Sometimes, too, out-of-school employment, coupled with its money-earning opportunities, seems more stimulating and more worthwhile than the harder-to-conceive long-range possibilities of a planned educational program. This is particularly true for students who are attending schools that are not making the school program stimulating and are not helping students recognize the present and future satisfactions and values of education.

During the past few years, however, there have been changes in the rigid pattern of separating a student's school life from his out-of-school life. Many schools and other youth-serving institutions have found reasons that have persuaded or even compelled them to take advantage of the energy and enthusiasm that the entrepreneurial role stimulates in many students. Entrepreneurial programs of many types have originated in these schools and institutions; often they have been developed under the guiding influence of students themselves. Here are a few examples:

☐ Home economics students at Jefferson High School in Portland, Oregon, have established a restaurant that is open for lunch five days a week and serves both students and teachers. A chef supervises the kitchen, and the home economics teacher supervises the entire operation. The dining area is a classroom converted by students into a pleasing, relaxing place with tables, chairs, linen and crockery that the students purchased. Students select the menus and prepare the food as well as performing all the other functions of a restaurant—keeping accounts, cleaning the kitchen and eating area and so forth.

☐ The Bedford Pines Buttermilk Bottom's Buying Club was initiated by young people and housewives living in an impoverished part of Atlanta, Georgia. Housewives had noted that different grocery stores in their part of the city charged very different prices for the same items. Working with high school students whose help they requested, they made a list of the most commonly purchased items such as eggs, milk and detergents. The students took the list from store to store and compared prices for each item. The results of their survey showed that prices for the same item varied by as much as one hundred and fifty percent. The students then made this information available throughout the community. Community members who had previously been apathetic about the problem were greatly angered when they discovered that their friendly corner grocer, who often gave popsicles to their children, was overcharging them. Working with the American Friends Service Committee, the students and adults figured out where they could buy these items in quantity at wholesale prices. They then, in effect, set up a cooperative by taking everyone's order to a wholesaler and buying the items for the neighborhood all at once at considerable savings.

☐ Rent-a-Kid grew out of the West End Neighborhood Development Center in Atlanta, Georgia. High school students desperately needed summer jobs. The staff of the Center suggested they set up and advertise a service whereby anyone wishing part-time help could call a central number to get a young person to help. The city media willingly aided the young people by advertising their availability. Kids themselves manned the phones. Businesses and individuals who needed their lawns cut, cars washed, or odd jobs done kept the phones ringing all summer.

These programs are merely representative of an expanding number of projects for student entrepreneurs. The benefits from these programs extend to everyone involved. Students benefit from participating in learning programs that relate to their personal hopes and plans, and they become more attentive students as they get a clearer idea of the contributions an organized educational program can make to the realization of their current and future aspirations.

Schools benefit by reexamining their programs to determine what is effective and what needs to be changed—both in content and in teaching methods. Schools, and students too, benefit by finding opportunities to stimulate the interest of teachers who have become bored with a traditional program and irritated by—or immune to—its failure to elicit enthusiastic responses from students. Schools also benefit by becoming more open to the creative ideas and youthful energy of teachers just entering the profession.

Communities benefit by a student program that makes vital goods and services available—often at reduced prices.

Everyone profits by having students, the school, and the community working together to explore and develop new and effective ways to be mutually helpful.

It would be unrealistic to assume that there are no dissenters, no problems, no calculated efforts to discourage the development of new ideas, or no honest convictions that the old order should not be disturbed. But one of the most significant advantages of involving young people and adults in the development of youth-related programs is the need to identify and solve the problems that are bound to arise. Not all ideas are feasible, no matter how much enthusiasm supports them. Ideas have to be evaluated; priorities have to be determined; the skills of problem-solving have to be learned; the influence of personality factors has to be recognized and dealt with; the possibility of failure has to be anticipated; the ability and willingness to accept the validity of some failures have to be evolved. These are not negative factors; they are vital, realistic aspects of learning.

The remainder of this chapter describes three projects that have successfully involved students as entrepreneurs.

MULTIPLE BUSINESS ENTERPRISES
MANUAL HIGH SCHOOL, DENVER, COLORADO

Manual is a high school in downtown Denver with a student population of nearly two thousand. Two-thirds of the students are black, and most of them would be classified as disadvantaged. Over the years they have reflected the attitudes and the behavior of most students who attend schools of the poor and the powerless: they have been reluctant to go to school; wary about caring enough to become involved; skeptical about any real value the school has to offer them; quick to "fail" and quick to drop out when the time arises.

A few years ago Manual High School acquired a new principal—a determined man who could not abide the status quo and who would not acknowledge despair. One of his first goals was to win the confidence of parents. He wanted to convince parents that Manual's educational purpose was not limited to preparing its students for a "trade" and to persuade them that the school could and would open the way to other educational opportunities as well. With support from the school staff, he insisted that Manual High School include a strong academic program. This helped greatly to win the confidence of the parents and give them hope that the school could offer new opportunities for their children. Students, too, could see that an educational program that would make them eligible for higher education could broaden their career prospects.

A second goal—equally important—was to incorporate into the vocational curriculum some training in the managerial and entrepreneurial aspects of various trades. Barriers to nonwhite youths in the skilled trades are great, but the barriers that limit their access to commerce and to business management are even greater. The principal reasoned that background in these areas would improve students' job qualifications, increase their chances for eventual employment—

including self-employment—and provide greater opportunities for promotion on a job.

Still a third goal is best expressed in the principal's own words:

"We feel that education starts in the community, that we learn in the community, and that we shall be doing something for the community.

This statement reveals a recognition of the intimate connection between the capacities of students to learn and the need for a sense of belonging to a "good" community.

House Construction

The first moment of fruition for the school's goals came on a cold January day when the title to a new house, constructed on a plot of Denver urban renewal land, passed to a large local family (twelve members) who had been top bidder among sixteen families who wanted the house. The family was excited and proud, but no more so than the Manual High School vocational arts students were when they passed title to the new owners. To the students this was "their" house. It was a full-size, brick-veneer, tri-level home. It had four bedrooms, three baths, living room, dining area, full basement, and a two-car garage. It was well designed and well constructed—and students at Manual had built it themselves.

In fact, Manual High School students were responsible for virtually every phase of the long process that turned a small, desolate parcel of Denver's inner city into a good dwelling for a large family. The principal and his staff may have provided the initial stimulus, but the students themselves quickly adopted the project.

A group of carpentry, masonry, and electricity students were the first to be involved. They formed the Manual High School Realty Corporation with the intention of building a house. Valuable help came from a teacher at Manual who was also a part-time realtor and from a Denver construction company that agreed to sponsor the project. As an initial safeguard, this construction company agreed to complete construction if Manual High School students were unable to finish the project.

Next, the Realty Corporation bid on urban renewal land and acquired a plot close to the school. On behalf of the students, the principal signed for a $16,000 loan from a Denver bank. FHA approvals were obtained, and by early spring construction was ready to proceed.

The students at Manual High School formed three more companies to implement their project. The Architectural Company worked on the design of the building; the Manual Accounting Company reviewed the bills, paid them, and maintained the books; the Thunderbolt Construction Company was created to do the actual house building. The companies included seventy-five high school juniors—white, Mexican-American, and black. Under faculty sponsorship, Manual High School students served as corporate officers in all these business organizations and made whatever significant decisions had to be made.

The students also did the hard physical labor of constructing the house. Twenty-six local labor unions cooperated on the project, and a union carpenter worked full time in the Manual High School classrooms to supplement the instruction of the regular industrial arts teachers. But every bit of the construction, except bricklaying, was actually done by students. Students laid foundations and built walls; they wired and plumbed and painted; they laid carpets. A number of construction companies allowed students to use their latest and most elaborate equipment—equipment that most vocational high schools just cannot afford. This helped to insure that the skills students acquired and the jobs they learned to do would not be obsolete nor out of line with what might be

Students work side by side with a professional roofer shingling "their" house.   MANUAL HIGH SCHOOL, DENVER, CO.

anticipated by the time they entered the employment market.

In their English classes, the vocational students drafted the contracts and handled the correspondence their house building required. Problems related to construction were dealt with in mathematics classes.

Actual construction took place both during school time and in the summer. During the school year students received academic credit; in the summer they were paid wages from funds supplied by a federal grant under ESEA Title I and the Neighborhood Youth Corps.

The house was ultimately sold for $2,000 less than the Realty Corporation's out-of-pocket costs, but the financial discrepancy between building costs and selling price is no measure of the educational value of the project. Skills were acquired, attitudes were changed, and energies were redirected. The practical value of understanding mathematics, for example, was perfectly clear to students who were using geometry to determine how to cut a rafter and arithmetical skills to estimate costs, check bills, and keep accurate records.

Many students gained new respect for themselves and new hope for the future as they discovered that business management was not beyond their grasp nor their range of aspirations. Some students discovered they possessed marketable skills or had acquired them; others discovered lines of work they might want to engage in later. Still others discovered (and this is an equally important discovery) that there were some kinds of work they would definitely want to avoid in the future.

It seems clear that the students who worked on the house developed new and deeper bonds among themselves and between themselves and the school and their community. Evidence for this conclusion is considerable: the house-building students had better attendance than the college-bound segment of Manual High School. Even though the program was organized so that the percentage of those judged to be potential dropouts was higher than the percentage of potential dropouts in the school as a whole, the percentage of actual dropouts among those working on the house project was lower than the school average. Moreover, there is strong evidence that the spirit of the whole school and the whole community was positively affected by the house-building project. It is also significant to note that not a single act of vandalism was committed against the Manual High School house during the entire period of its construction. During the same period, other building projects in the neighborhood experienced serious problems with vandals.

Urban Renewal Contracts

The house construction project led Manual High School into still bigger projects. The urban renewal activity that surrounds Manual on four sides is a major undertaking. The Denver Urban Renewal Authority (DURA) has determined that thirty-two square blocks are to be totally rehabilitated. Several hundred residents will be affected, and millions of tax dollars have been committed to the ten-year project. At some point after students at Manual High School had begun constructing their house, a black instructor at the school asked why all these millions of dollars should go to white building construction workers—people who each night left the inner city and went to their suburban homes. He urged Manual students to try to establish the fact that they could make responsible use of a share of the project money. Meanwhile, the Denver Urban Renewal Authority became sensitive to the fact that Manual High School was the last remaining stable social institution in the renewal area and concluded that support from the school might help to increase local acceptance.

Manual High School officials were cautious about cooperating with the urban renewal authorities despite their desire to find remunerative community work for the students. They knew that urban renewal had often resulted in pushing poor nonwhite residents out and moving white middle-class businesses in. After careful investigation, however, they concluded that this particular urban renewal project would really help Manual's community. The project is strictly residential neighborhood renewal, focusing on new or rehabilitated housing, parks, streets, and sidewalks. A great deal of community control has been built into the project, and a number of Housing and Urban Development (HUD) regulations, applicable within the project, are designed to eliminate absentee landlords in favor of local owners.

With the skills and experience they had achieved through building and selling a house, Manual High School students had confidence in their potential for coping with the responsibilities that would be involved, and they decided to compete for a wide variety of urban renewal contracts.

The four student companies that jointly worked on Manual's house gave way to a new organization, Creative Urban Living Environment (CULE). The first function of CULE was to secure a contract with Denver's urban renewal authorities. It came away with $61,000 in contracts and the likelihood of receiving much more. Among the jobs contracted for were the rehabilitation of at least fifteen houses, the design of four mini-parks, the installation of twenty-one blocks of sidewalk, and the publication of a bulletin explaining to local residents their options under the urban renewal program.

Students themselves have done all the contracting. They have also taken on the task of examining all of DURA's decisions carefully to assure that the welfare of the local community is not being jeopardized. CULE's major accomplishments so far have been in design, but rehabilitation of the first of the fifteen houses has been completed, and some sidewalks have been laid. Denver city inspectors have called the sidewalks "A—" work; one inspector said the students lay the best sidewalks in town.

CULE has bought a dump truck and a loader on the strength of a $6,000 bank loan, and the faculty coordinator for the project believes that CULE is now the only contractor, based actually within the urban renewal community, that is capable of performing major construction jobs. When outside professionals are called in for a specific job, they are required not only to do the job but also to teach students how it is done. Students are paid by the hour for their summer work with CULE and are covered by Workman's Compensation and Social Security. Students do ninety-seven percent of the work themselves; the faculty coordinator's main job is to help raise enough money so that the young people will be able to do what needs to be done.

It is the hope of Manual High School administrators that every department in the school will eventually be involved in some phase of the urban renewal project. Art and drafting classes have already designed the mini-parks; sociology classes have been assigned the task of explaining urban renewal to local residents. The total number of students thus far actively involved in the project ranges between eighty and ninety, and faculty members would like to see that number increase.

Day Care Center

Another Manual High School innovation has been a day care center located at a nearby junior high school that has been operating since April 1971. The center accepts no fees and therefore cannot be said to be operating on a business basis; nevertheless, it provides student participants with firsthand experiences in a field that is likely to be important in an entrepreneurial sense and is also full of possibilities for personal growth. At the same time the day care center endeavors to provide an important service to the Manual High School neighborhood and to develop the ability of students to relate to young children.

At any one time, twelve Manual High School students—sophomores and juniors—are enrolled in the program. Participants are selected on the basis of demonstrated interest, and a survey course called Home Economics and Related Occupations (HERO) is a prerequisite. Entering students begin the program with a six-week training course. The day care center operates mornings only; in the afternoon there is a special class for program members. Full school credit is granted for participation in the day care program.

Beneficiaries of the program are twenty-nine young children, ages two to four years, all from Manual's immediate neighborhood. The faculty coordinator of the program is pleased with the progress thus far and especially with the helpfulness and responsiveness of the parents of the young children being supervised. Her main concern right now is expansion. She would like to run a full-day program that would offer substantially greater opportunity to deal with nutritional problems, but the costs involved make such expansion impossible right now.

Preprofessional Program

Still another innovation at Manual High School has been the practice of allowing large numbers of students—six hundred or more, most of them seniors—to spend two school periods a day for at least one semester in firsthand observation of a professional career in which they think they might be interested. Often there is no immediate financial remuneration for students in this program because the professions they are interested in are too complex to allow a novice to participate in them actively enough to warrant substantial financial benefits. Nevertheless, there is a good deal of real student participation built into the program with obvious long-range benefits.

The professions include engineering, law, aero-space education, and various forms of communication. Students in the pre-engineering program use laboratories at Denver University while taking college courses and earning college credits. Students in the prelaw program visit courts, prepare contracts for school projects, and work with the local Legal Aid Society. Students in the aero-space program become acquainted particularly with skills and opportunities in the aviation construction and maintenance fields. Local resource personnel from aircraft manufacturers and from technical and flight schools work with this group. Preeducation students work in nearby elementary schools. Students in the precommunication program are assigned to a radio station, to a television channel, or to one of the Denver newspapers.

The preprofessional program was originally designed to challenge the frequent boredom of graduating seniors with potential real-life work experiences. It was soon discovered, however, that younger students could also benefit by exposure to careers that lay outside their ordinary range of experience. One of Manual's most interesting preprofessional programs, the premedical one, is aimed not at seniors but at juniors and even sophomores. The program takes account of the fact that relatively few blacks and Mexican-Americans go into science and medicine and undertakes to change that situation by exposing students to these professions at an age when high school chemistry and advanced mathematics courses still lie potentially ahead of them. It seems quite evident that a student who gains confidence in his science capacities in high school will be more likely to pursue science studies in college and in later life.

The coordinator of the premedical program actually prefers to take students with less than a B average. It is these students, he believes, who are most in need of motivation to identify and develop their potential. Expression of genuine interest in the premedical program is one prerequisite for application; one semester of biology is another. The school-time program itself lasts for one semester, with meetings each morning of the week for one-and-a-half hours. The program can handle only twenty-five students at any one time; of these, approximately forty percent come from high schools other than Manual. The inclusion of other students is a generous gesture on the part of Manual, but one result is that there are always some qualified Manual High School applicants who cannot be accommodated.

The morning of a student enrolled in the Manual High School premedical program can be interesting indeed. At nine o'clock a bus arrives at the high school to take him and his fellow students to the medical school of Colorado University where the bulk of his instruction takes place. On the bus he may hear recorded lectures or he may listen to a "live" lecture from the coordinator. When students arrive at the medical school, they may hear a lab technician or a family-care nurse explain their jobs. They may see a demonstration by a doctor of exactly what must be done to a human baby immediately after it is born. One day a student may be part of a small group that visits a hospital ward; another day he may observe organs from one animal being surgically transplanted into the body of another, different kind of animal. Some days he may simply study out of his textbook, preparing himself for future experiences at the University or follow up on past ones. At the very beginning of the semester the student spends two weeks studying general science principles. Toward the end of the semester he will probably dissect an animal. Seventy-two different topics are presented to him in one semester, and every six weeks he helps to evaluate the program of which he is a part.

At the end of the semester, the premedical program doesn't necessarily end for the student. During each year of the program's existence, the coordinator has secured from private foundations or from federal government programs money to provide summer medical service jobs for many of the students. Some have worked at Colorado General Hospital; others have worked in the neighborhood health offices of the Model Cities program. Several students have maintained contacts with their summer employers after graduating from Manual and while going on to college, and in the summer they return to an interesting medical position.

The results of the premedical program have been highly gratifying: the rate of absenteeism among premedical students is far lower than the school's average; nine or ten of the first twelve students are now in college pursuing premedical or other science programs. The coordinator's major problem is that more students would like to participate, but limited quarters at Colorado University make expansion difficult.

Manual's premedical program has received extraordinary cooperation: doctors and nurses have been uniformly generous in offering their time and services, and the University of Colorado has supplied a wide range of facilities and services without cost.

In the aero-space program, students participate in a curriculum that seeks to develop skills and creative abilities and also to develop awareness of the related importance of such studies as mathematics, physics, and earth sciences. Through a hands-on shop experience of actually constructing an aircraft, students develop skills in welding, woodworking, electrical wiring, hydraulics, sheet metal fabrication, blueprint reading, weight and balance problems, and engine installation procedures. The students have completed one specially designed aerobatic biplane and have had the satisfaction of flying with their instructor in the plane they built.

Students who participate in the aero-space program have a knowledgeable basis for deciding whether or not this vocational area is for them. A number of graduates have gone on to continue their education in the aero-space field—some to technical schools and some to colleges.

This preprofessional program, like other such programs at Manual, has received excellent support from appropriate local resources. In fact, practically all of the school's innovative projects have had comparable support. But it is important to point out that the cooperation Manual High School has received has come about in large measure because the school has earned the respect of the entire Denver community through its own dedication to its students and its efforts to make a difference in the lives of young people and the community.

SOUL GATE SHOPPING CENTER
CLEVELAND, OHIO

Not every entrepreneurial program has been as extensive or as durable as the projects developed at Manual High School in Denver. The Soul Gate Shopping Center of the Franklin Delano Roosevelt Junior High School, located in the Glenville area of Cleveland, operated for only one summer, but during that time it performed brilliantly.

Glenville is a black urban neighborhood with a population that includes people on welfare, people who are working but are at or near poverty levels, and people who belong to the middle class. Opportunities for summer employment of teenagers are limited. The principal and the faculty of Franklin Delano Roosevelt Junior High School had given much thought to ways in which the school might help to provide stimulating and constructive vacation-time activities for thirteen- and fourteen-year-olds—young people who might otherwise simply kill time or actually get into serious trouble. For example:

What would it take to make the basic learning skills palatable to youngsters who often seem indifferent to most kinds of instructional programs in the school?

What kinds of training would be of most immediate benefit to FDR's students?

How could FDR contribute to developing in its students

some of the pride that comes from helping to control their own day-to-day living?

Solutions to some of the questions developed over a number of years. Several teachers of FDR's apparently less gifted students used factory-type projects to provide a setting where students would be motivated to use reading, writing, and mathematics to deal with concrete problems. In one class, for example, the students developed a business—making paper flowers, ash trays and knickknacks for the home—and sold shares of stock to obtain money for purchasing basic supplies such as clay and plaster of paris.

In January 1970, FDR was informed by the Cleveland central education office that the school would be free to make whatever arrangements it desired for a summer school. The principal developed the idea of a shopping center where students would actually operate their own small businesses throughout the summer, experiencing the routine day-to-day obligations of business life along with the heady but sometimes frustrating moments of decision-making. He drew up a list of small businesses that might lend themselves to student participation because (*1*) they could operate within or from the school building itself, (*2*) they would require little capital investment, and (*3*) they would call for skills that novices could acquire quickly. He passed his list on to the faculty for their reactions and recommendations.

The list then went to the student body as a whole. Students surveyed community business needs, made recommendations on the basis of what they discovered, and then voted on the various suggestions.

Fourteen businesses for the Soul Gate Shopping Center were selected:

1. Claywood Production was to make clay and wood artifacts
2. D's Type It To Ya was to do typing
3. Soulville Landscaping

4. Stop-n-Shop Gift Mart
5. Tot & Teen Nursery
6. Wayout Advertising Agency
7. Soul Gate Printing
8. Soul Gate Shopping News
9. Soul Soundwave, a singing group
10. Jet Spray Window Wash
11. P.D.Q. Car Wash
12. BS's Rustic Rendezvous Country Restaurant
13. Shonuff Thang, an entertainment agency
14. Soul City Bank, which was to handle the major financial transactions of the other thirteen businesses

The Soul Gate Shopping Center opened when the summer session started. Two hundred and sixty students, most of them thirteen- and fourteen-year-olds, enrolled in the program. Some of them enrolled to make up courses failed during the school year; Soul Gate was a basic part of the summer school curriculum, and credit was earned for participation in it. The majority of the enrollees, however, were involved for the possibility of learning from the experience and making some money at the same time. Obviously, the enrollment represented a broad range of abilities and prior achievements.

In the morning classes taught skills related to the businesses being operated; in the afternoon the businesses conducted their operations. A faculty member and a teacher's aide were always present during the business hours of each group, but students carried out all the important tasks.

At the beginning of the summer session, the students in each business elected officers and sold shares of stock in the enterprise. Parents, neighbors, and other students were canvassed, and the participants themselves commonly bought shares in their own companies. Shares sold for one dollar and most of the stock sales raised between $50 and $100. This was enough to buy the basic supplies—brushes, brooms, paints, or whatever was needed for a particular operation.

Soul Gate proved to be extremely popular. Its biggest customers were the students themselves, but faculty members found the Tot and Teen Nursery to be a useful service, and many local merchants found it worthwhile to advertise in the *Soul Gate Shopping News*.

Soul Gate was designed to run for one summer session—from the beginning of June until the end of July. As the closing weeks approached, the fourteen businesses of Soul Gate organized a parade to show the residents of the Glenville neighborhood what they had achieved. All kinds of floats and displays were prepared. The Shonuff Thang Entertainment Agency put its band and dancers on a float. The *Shopping News* had its reporters out on the streets in costumes made of newspapers, handing out copies of their paper as they marched. The Wayout Advertising Agency built a rocket filled with brochures; the rocket was set to take off when it reached the judges' stand. The parade was a grand occasion, filled with enthusiasm of both participants and spectators, and it seemed to symbolize the spirit of Soul Gate. Shortly thereafter all the businesses were liquidated. Finally, accountings were made, and it was discovered that every business had made a profit, from the $22.74 net of the Wayout Advertising Agency to the $215.50 of the Jet Spray Window Wash. Profits were distributed to shareholders—and then came some remarkable bonuses.

The principal had procured $20,000 from the Mayor's Youth Council and the George Gund Foundation. When the summer session was over, the money was given to Soul Gate's student workers, who had received no wages for their efforts; the amounts of money were commensurate with their productivity. All participants with satisfactory attendance records were paid a base bonus of $120 for the six weeks. An amount reckoned on the relative profits of each concern (this ranged from a few dollars to almost a hundred) was added to the base bonus. A worker in the Jet Spray Window Wash, for example, might have earned more than $200 for his efforts.

Just as important as their financial earnings—and more important in the long run—was the learning that took place during one short summer. Tests conducted at the program's conclusion showed that most of the participants had not only learned a practical work skill but had also improved their business vocabulary and their mathematics skills.

Soul Gate was not continued the following summer for several reasons: it had required a tremendous amount of extra effort on the part of everyone—especially the faculty; during the following fall some problems cropped up—notably, extra money had to be raised to cover some checks that the Soul City Bank had mistakenly written; the principal who had originated the idea left FDR, and the new principal decided not to continue the program.

In retrospect, the principal who initiated the idea has especially fond memories of the Jet Spray Window Washers. It was they, he believes, who somehow crystallized the fine spirit of Soul Gate. It was not merely that they made the greatest profits; it was how they made these profits. They kept their expenses down to the second lowest of any of the businesses, and they worked very hard, without extravagance or publicity. What the principal remembers with such satisfaction is the spirit of the window washers. They were among the very youngest boys to work at Soul Gate, and their equipment was often oversized for them. When they marched out into the neighborhood with their pails and brushes and poles, they looked like a midget army. They rang bells and knocked on doors and didn't take "no" for an answer; they *wanted* to wash people's windows! They were enthusiastic, and they were proud. These are the qualities the principal is pleased to think that Soul Gate inspired. As one of the Jet Spray Window Washers wrote:

While earning money I really realized that money was hard to get but easy to spend and it is better to put in long hours. I was proud, too, because we had no complaints about our work.

SOUL-MOBILE RECORD SHOP
WASHINGTON, D.C.

By no means all of the nation's recently developed student entrepreneurial projects have actually been operated by schools. Many that could be adapted to a school program have been initiated by other youth-serving institutions or by individuals.

The Soul-Mobile Record Shop is one example. The shop is located in Lansburgh Park, a section of Washington that is often considered by its residents to be a forgotten area. The area is not truly middle class, but neither is it as desperately poor and ravaged as some other parts of Washington where Model Cities money and other funds have gone.

Some years ago a D.C. public school teacher who believed that the city recreation centers in the southwest offered insufficient facilities for youngsters in the neighborhood, founded Troyce's Corner Youth Center. She acquired a record player, a billiard table, and a few other pieces of equipment, and soon the Center became a popular place.

Before long, some of the students came to her with a suggestion. Since there was no really adequate record shop in the southwest where they could readily buy records, why couldn't students start a record shop themselves? The teacher thought well of her young friends' idea, and went out to see if she could find the money needed to turn their hopes into a reality. She obtained enough money from the Washington office of the Community Development Foundation to buy a forty-six foot by ten foot trailer to house the shop. From the Mayor's Youth Unit she secured a smaller sum to purchase the initial stock of records.

The Soul-Mobile Record Shop opened in June 1969 and is operated six days a week, staying open every week night until 8:00 p.m. It sells rock, soul, jazz, and blues including 45s and LPs—all at discount prices. In addition, it has expanded its stock so that it is now something of a variety shop with other items for sale. In spite of its slight expansion, one of the most fascinating characteristics of the shop is that it is still such a *small* operation. It employs only two young people at a time. They are paid an hourly wage and, on the average, have worked in the shop for a year or a year and a half. The employees have been uniformly young—twelve to fifteen years old—and the teacher has tried to select workers from students who would not be eligible for Neighborhood Youth Corps jobs. The young people perform all the tasks required to operate a record shop: they check inventory, keep books, sell records, and select new stock. Many of them have become very skillful in handling these managerial tasks. The teacher who works with the shop believes that one of the employees, a thirteen-year-old girl, could run the shop all by herself if she ever had to!

Perhaps the most remarkable thing about the Soul-Mobile Record Shop is that it is completely self-supporting. No funding has recently come from any outside source. The reason that Soul-Mobile can stay in business is that it still serves a legitimate commercial need in the neighborhood. For one thing, a purchaser can save a lot of carfare by buying his records at Soul-Mobile rather than in the stores downtown.

Even so, Soul-Mobile has financial problems. Its fostering organization, Troyce's Corner Youth Center, is now defunct, driven out of existence by drug addiction in the neighborhood. The record shop itself had to close down once after several burglaries had depleted its resources. The phone has sometimes been disconnected. The single old heater that provides Soul-Mobile's warmth through the winter months is broken, and there are no funds for replacement. To all but the fostering teacher and the student workers, the future of Soul-Mobile might seem bleak. But to those who have really given of themselves to the shop, there are many consolations: several alumni of Soul-Mobile have gone on to take up business administration—two of them are already at the college level; the shop still provides an important service to the youth of its community; and the manner of Soul-Mobile's survival is enough to make everyone connected with it proud of both its learning and the earning achievements. Soul-Mobile has survived through sheer profit-making activity, despite all the problems and costs involved in educating young people in the techniques of business enterprise.

A FURTHER WORD

In Denver, Cleveland, and Washington, the benefits that have accrued to those involved in student entrepreneurial projects have followed strikingly familiar patterns—in general, the pattern outlined at the beginning of this chapter. Students' eagerness to participate in projects that are realistic to them has provided motivation for learning and for staying in school through high school and beyond. The fostering organizations have found satisfaction in these results and have learned much about how to evaluate and modify educational programs to make them more challenging and more effective.

Student interest at Manual High School in Denver is evident in such concrete forms as increased attendance rates and decreased dropout rates. At Soul Gate, student interest revealed itself in similar ways. Furthermore, during the period of Soul Gate's operation, there were practically no discipline problems.

In contrast to Manual High School and Franklin Delano Roosevelt Junior High School, Soul-Mobile has suffered from vandalism and burglary. But the rebound capacity of this small organization—and even its constructive use of difficulties—cannot be overestimated. When a youngster responsible for several burglaries at the shop was caught, he was hired for the Soul-Mobile staff. There hasn't been a burglary since. This does not mean that this one youngster was responsible for most of the burglaries, but it certainly points up the influence of positive rather than punitive action. The fact that Soul-Mobile has survived its parent organization, Troyce's Corner Youth Center, speaks for itself.

All three projects have provided student participants with learning that has been of immediate and obvious value to them. The fact that students recognize a relationship between what is learned and how it can be put to use is reflected not merely—or even primarily—in the money they earn but rather in the fact that many students have gone on to acquire further education in fields to which they were first exposed in projects in which they participated. The three communities in which these projects were based have all received tangible benefits from the entrepreneurial programs. All the projects have, of course, faced problems. But there are some very practical solutions to the problems that developed. For example, adult supervisors must see to it that, when the situation warrants, all the anti-burglary precautions of any business enterprise are taken. Adult supervisors must be particularly watchful over accounting tasks since they are among the most difficult everyday business tasks to perform—not only for students but for adults as well—and since errors in this area are among the potentially most disastrous to a business.

It should be noted that while there are some practical remedies available, these problems point to another difficulty that is not so easy to deal with. This is the problem of financing.

Financing is a basic concern for all business enterprises but it is particularly troublesome for student entrepreneur programs. It is simply not reasonable to expect these programs to operate on a true profit basis. Take Manual's CULE, for example. CULE lays excellent sidewalks, but it cannot lay them nearly as quickly as another firm could since its workers must learn as they work. Yet CULE pays each student worker a reasonable wage to maintain his morale—an integral part of the educational process. As things now stand, a program for student entrepreneurs must perform at least two jobs; the businesses with which it may compete have to perform only one. To compete with an established business, a student program must do a job at the standard price; to achieve its long-range educational purpose, the project must teach the students *how to do* the job—and that involves developing related skills that may never have seemed significant to a student before. This in itself is a value that is probably of more enduring worth than the financial success of a student enterprise. It is doubtful, in fact, that the value of a given project should be assessed with great emphasis on financial profit. When a school performs its related educational tasks, a project almost inevitably, and justifiably, winds up costing more money than can be charged for the job that is being done.

Aside from these problems, the experience of the programs in Denver, Cleveland, and Washington suggests at least three requisites to the success of similar programs elsewhere. The first of these is extraordinary dedication, ability, and flexibility on the part of the faculty members connected with the project. The programs are so different from traditional classroom routines that they almost invariably require vast expenditures of teacher time. Students may themselves conduct all the ordinary business operations, but the dedication of the students in no way exempts the faculty from assuring that the program operates continually for the maximum benefit of its participants. Soul Gate's teachers put in far more hours each day than did teachers in the rest of FDR's summer school program. Each business required classes in the morning and then long hours of operations in the afternoon during which faculty presence in the background contributed to confidence and to a sense of expanding competence on the part of the students. Obviously, too, the teacher working with Soul-Mobile has put in tremendously long hours.

But time is only one ingredient. Principals and teachers who have rigid ideas about what constitutes a good instructional program are skeptical about change. Flexibility, the capacity to see alternative ways of achieving educational objectives, the willingness to experiment, the security to try something that may fail, the ability to analyze and evaluate, and the stamina to keep trying—these are personality ingredients that are vital. Fortunately, their presence in a few individuals can often provide the stimulus and the leadership needed to attract the support of the more traditionally oriented educator. Manual High School offers such an example. The principal is sensitive, dynamic, and intensely dedicated. The faculty at Manual has a number of exceptionally unorthodox and persistent teachers who make a tremendous difference. In several cases these are people who have highly specialized and saleable skills. They could be making much more money working in the business world, but they choose to work at Manual instead, passing on to students their unusual and practically indispensable skills.

A second requisite for success is some degree of community cooperation. In Washington community cooperation was responsible for getting a trailer and a shop site in federally controlled Lansburgh Park. Community cooperation supported the Soul Gate grand parade—perhaps the high mark of the program's success.

Denver's contributions to Manual High School are numerous indeed. They include the use of equipment from construction companies, instruction from union journeymen, bank loans, and a press that has given much favorable publicity to the school. Such support is necessary for student entrepreneur programs that need the kinds of skills and equipment the business world possesses and the schools do not—and perhaps should not. It is much more economical for businesses to supply facilities out of their surpluses than it is for schools to borrow or purchase such facilities on the open market. The latter course would make prohibitive the cost of nearly all realistic student entrepreneur programs. For a school, the challenge is to make its goals sufficiently attractive and its interest sufficiently obvious to persuade community business and labor groups that the cultivation of skills in potential employees and the goodwill generated by providing men and supplies will, in terms of sheer good business sense, ultimately outweigh whatever immediate costs are involved.

A third requisite for success is to avoid getting into a rut and to be always open to change. This requisite was alluded to by the former principal of FDR Junior High when he once spoke of what he would have done with Soul Gate had he stayed on at the school. He said he would have tried to keep the program going for three summers. In the fourth summer he would have changed it, substituting something new and fresh, something designed to teach the same skills but different enough to reinvigorate students, faculty, and the community.

Keeping fresh remains a challenge that all programs will have to meet if they are to survive, for they are unorthodox programs that are designed to educate by meeting immediate and sometimes fleeting needs and desires. If keeping fresh is a requisite of successful education generally, it is doubly so for projects such as these, which depend so much for their very existence on a high level of school motivation.

There are four aspects of offering students an entrepreneurial experience that may cause concern in the minds of people dedicated to "liberal" education. They may raise unsettling questions about the functions of the schools.

1. If schools are going to start incorporating businesses into their curriculum, would it be better and more efficient to send

students straight out into the real business world and let businesses do their own job training?

2. Are entrepreneurial programs depriving students of an important component of high school education—an exposure to culture that is detached from the commercial world and capable of enlarging minds in ways that may ultimately yield enjoyment and satisfaction that dollars can never match?

3. Is it sound educational policy to pay students to learn?

4. If the values are as great as they are claimed to be, why are so many of the programs geared largely to black students? What are the possible effects on attitudes of whites and blacks? Are these programs still another indication of previous oppression and continuing discrimination?

One response to the first question is this: businesses train people only in those aspects of work that are of immediate benefit to the business. One can hardly expect business to train sixteen-year-olds in any but the lesser, chiefly manual skills. A major objective of Manual High School's programs is to teach students *managerial* as well as *manual* skills—managerial skills few business enterprises would find reason to teach to high school students. All of Manual High School's trade programs now contain a large academic component for the very purpose of assuring that Manual's students will eventually become eligible for jobs the business world today would commonly suppose them to be incapable of handling, and would not take time to discover if this supposition was correct. Soul-Mobile and Soul Gate also taught managerial skills, and related academic skills were well integrated with the Soul Gate summer curriculum.

A partial answer to the second question has already been given. None of the programs described in this chapter have abandoned their commitment to academic education. At Manual High School that commitment has been strengthened. Moreover, none of these programs was designed to operate exclusive of other school programs. No student spends all his school time in any one entrepreneurial program; there is time left for history and literature and other areas of study. Furthermore, most of the entrepreneurial programs have arisen out of situations where students in traditional classrooms were simply not learning and were prime candidates for dropping out and ensuing problems.

In response to the third question, one could point out first of all that students are not being paid money directly for "learning"; they are being paid for work that normally commands a wage. One can go further and plead for an open mind on the subject of payment. Right now there are a number of experimental programs operating where students are, in fact, given direct monetary rewards for acquiring basic academic skills. The results of such experiments, especially their long-term effects on morale and on learning motivation in the schools, are not yet known. In the meantime, it would seem prudent not to condemn programs where money is used as an indirect incentive.

If the first questions have been adequately answered, then the response to the fourth concern should fall into place. Entrepreneurial programs are not instruments of cultural oppression. The fact that entrepreneurial programs have developed primarily in heavily black schools and neighborhoods reflects nothing more than an assertion of local priorities over other less sensitive ones just as does the fact that adult blacks have been largely responsible for the development and administration of the programs.

One of the greatest assets these entrepreneurial programs possess is the pride and enthusiasm they develop in their young participants. If such programs can continue to evoke that pride and enthusiasm, and if the students can continue to pass on these attitudes to the communities in which they live, then the practical problems of manpower, equipment, and money shortages that these programs naturally engender may well become manageable.

YOUTH

as community problem-solvers

My family has lived in this suburban middle-class area for seventeen years. We have seen the destruction of this beautiful area. . . . Well, we've got to change this. . . . So, when you get those little old ladies saving their bags for when they return to the market, then you know you're changing life styles.

TO ALL TENANTS
You have full rights to complain about any breakdown in service in your building and apartment—painting, plastering, plumbing . . . , sanitary conditions, etc. Any threats to evict you or increase your rent cannot be carried out. In fact, if lack of service continues, you may apply for a decrease in rent through the agencies of the City of New York.

All the houses have to be built around the park. I want everybody to look out and see trees.

These statements were made by some of the many young people who are concerned about the problems that exist in the communities in which they live. The first was made by a student who was helping to organize anti-pollution activities in Campolindo, California. The second quotes a sign put up by New York City young people who were fighting substandard housing. The third was the comment of a young boy who had been selected to be the architect of a papier-mâché model city project being constructed by his class in a New York City elementary school.

These quotations call attention to some of the many ways young people are trying to help solve problems they see in the world outside the school. Communities—all communities— would be wise to recognize and make use of the vital resources available in their young citizens. Young people are impatient. When they see a problem, and they get an idea about how to cope with it, they want action. Often their enthusiasm can carry them over obstacles that would discourage adults. And their optimism seems to accelerate their ability to develop skills necessary for dealing with problems. Added to enthusiasm and optimism are physical and mental energy and a remarkable capacity for single-minded dedication to something they feel is truly important. With support from the school and community, young people can develop and learn to use the problem-solving skills so desperately needed for coping with current and future social problems.

Most programs that involve students in community action have some basic steps in common: (1) the identification and selection of real community needs, (2) the appointment of school and community administrators who are sympathetic to the unique problems that youngsters are likely to encounter, and (3) the establishment of adequate training programs. The projects described in this chapter indicate some of the ways that young people, schools, and communities can together approach their particular problems.

EARTH—THE ECOLOGY MOVEMENT
MORAGA, CALIFORNIA

In the fall of 1969, before ecology became a household word, Campolindo High School in Moraga, California, near San Francisco, originated a unit entitled "What's Ecology?" It was part of the year-long American government course required of all California high school seniors. The unit was prepared by an ecologist in collaboration with a Campolindo social studies teacher and was taught by a three-man team. Students who took the course were deeply disturbed by what they learned about the pollution of their environment, and they were eager to find remedies. Many of them became even more disturbed and more eager for action when, at the suggestion of their teachers, they attended a number of conferences on the ecological crisis. At one of these conferences, a specialist in population biology alarmed them with his vivid predictions about the results of overpopulation. At another session, the Campolindo students and students from the University of California at Berkeley and elsewhere participated in discussions of ecology issues with internationally known environmentalists. From these experiences the students gained confidence that they actually could help rebalance and preserve the environment.

After the conferences a small group of students worked with three faculty members to organize what they called a "Smog-Free Locomotion Day" at Campolindo. They encouraged the entire school population *not* to drive on one specific day—December 4. The response was overwhelming. On December 4 the parking lot was virtually empty; sixteen hundred students and faculty members, some of whom lived as far as eighteen miles away, came by bicycle, tandem, horse, unicycle, wagon, roller skates, and on foot. All of them carried signs and some of them wore gas masks.

"Smog-Free Locomotion Day," well publicized by the San

Francisco-Oakland Bay area media, served as a natural springboard for students at Campolindo who wished to found an organization for environmental action. During the weeks following "Locomotion Day," the students and their three faculty advisors met frequently to discuss organizational alternatives. The students fiercely resisted forming a club; they wanted more flexibility and a broader base than a club could offer. At the same time, they realized the need for some kind of structure. After considering several options, they settled on a loose organization that came to be called EARTH —the Ecology Movement.

The organizational premise upon which EARTH was founded is flexibility. Nevertheless, a pattern exists. At the beginning of the school year, students interested in working with EARTH choose a specific committee to work with. Each committee then has a meeting of its new members and selects a chairman. Next the committee chairmen meet with a student coordinator who is elected by all of EARTH's volunteers. This group, called the Executive Committee, is responsible for making major decisions for the whole organization. A student may work on as many committees as he wants and for as many hours as he wants. If there is no committee doing what he wants to do, he can form a new committee himself. Each committee makes its own decisions about carrying out its program. Lines of communication are left open—any student in EARTH, or any student at Campolindo High School for that matter, may go directly to EARTH's tiny office with a suggestion or a plan. EARTH's office with its own telephone and its shelves stacked high with reports is really a clearinghouse for suggestions, plans, questions, and information.

EARTH has two faculty advisors, both teachers of the "What's Ecology?" unit. These advisors do not interfere with EARTH's decision-making processes unless an infringement of law or school policy arises—which is very seldom. Their main functions, as they perceive them, are to help students

A poster prepared by students to dramatize careless littering.
PETER KLEINBARD

make contacts in the adult communities of Moraga and the Bay area and to provide continuity. Since most of the students taking the ecology unit are seniors, it is the advisors with their intimate knowledge of the program who provide the necessary bridge from one year to the next and help to maintain continuity.

In the third year of the program's existence, two hundred and twenty-five students, representing many social outlooks and many intellectual accomplishments, came to the fall organizational meeting. During the year some of them contributed little, but many worked more than forty hours a week —after school, on weekends, and through the summer. Most of these students were seniors, but all of Campolindo's students, from grades nine through twelve, are eligible. At one time EARTH had twelve committees working in such areas as recycling, legislative action, and maintaining a speakers bureau. EARTH receives no funds whatever from the Campolindo schools, and the faculty advisors are not released from any of their other instructional responsibilities. EARTH's income, which is about $1,100 per month, comes from the sale of materials—glass, aluminum, and other metals—that have been reprocessed by the recycling equipment that EARTH purchased and is still paying for.

EARTH's diverse accomplishments have been impressive.

During its earliest days, at a conference held by the U.S. Department of the Interior's Federal Water Pollution Control Commission, EARTH representatives gave the assembled delegates a real shock. The students called attention to a federal law that limits the use of federal waters to owners of one hundred and sixty acres of land or less; they analyzed the implications of this law; and then they requested a congressional investigation to determine why the law was not being enforced. Their presentation was the most surprising one at the conference and it stirred up considerable controversy. Although this law remains unenforced, the Campolindo students opened many people's eyes to the opportunities already available for fighting the continuing misuse of natural resources.

Shortly after the Department of the Interior conference, EARTH sponsored the first Campolindo Community Ecology Education Workshop. This workshop became a prototype for several subsequent meetings that have helped educate the Campolindo community about ecological problems and their possible solutions. Speakers have included state lawmakers as well as scholars from diverse ecological fields.

EARTH participated in the formation of Students for Ecological Action (SEA), a loose communications network through which high school ecology groups in the San Francisco-Oakland Bay area try to coordinate their activities. In addition EARTH sends speakers to other schools and community organizations, answers phone and mail inquiries from local citizens with pollution problems, and publishes a pamphlet on recycling materials, ecology bibliographies, and pamphlets containing population statistics and listings of the relative biodegradability of detergents.

EARTH members have testified before state legislative committees on programs for environmental action.

During its first year of operation, EARTH recycled twenty-five hundred pounds of aluminum and a large amount of tin. With the purchase of new recycling equipment, which handles other metals and glass as well, the output is increasing. The community now recognizes this recycling operation as one solution of a significant community problem.

A number of other ecology-oriented activities at Campolindo, although they didn't originate in an EARTH committee, have become genuine parts of the movement because they have been of benefit to and have benefitted from EARTH's activities. Among these have been an American government class project to cultivate an organic garden on school grounds, studies of such subjects as water pollution and the biodegradability of various detergents, *Silent Spring*, a short film with an original score, and a smog-free electric motorcycle which was built by a group of physics and American government students under the direction of a physics teacher and entered in the Cal Tech-MIT Transcontinental Clean Air Race. One of the projects now underway in the Campolindo workshops is the construction of an electric car.

EARTH has received widespread and gratifying recognition for its efforts. Campolindo students have appeared repeatedly on Bay area television and radio programs; local newspapers have run features on their activities; and wire service reporters have interviewed them. One year EARTH won the Bay Area Council's Award of Merit in competition for the Bay Area Environmental Award. Perhaps most important, recognition has been high at the community level. Local citizens are constantly calling EARTH to ask questions and to make offers.

What is most gratifying to EARTH's students is the wide recognition they receive for their ability as problem-solvers. They are respected as persons who are able and willing to solve concrete problems, and who have an organization, a store of knowledge, and contacts that make them better able than most adults to accomplish things in the complex area of environmental protection. EARTH is taken seriously by the communities of which it is a part; student participants respond by taking themselves and their work seriously. EARTH's future looks bright.

It should be noted, too, that ecology has now found its way into the ninth-grade curriculum. The treatment is, of course, at a simpler level from that of the ecology component of the senior course in American government, but this early exposure may well provide EARTH with large numbers of knowledgeable students who can have three to four years to work with the ecology project.

A school district that wants to start something like EARTH

should keep in mind that a number of faculty members and students must commit themselves to spending long hours on the project. In some cases it may be necessary to hire a full-time program coordinator. Campolindo students and faculty advisors would say that what is most important is enthusiasm. They would also say that it seems wise policy for a school to build flexibility into its environmental protection program. Ecology is a vast and dynamic field that can generate innumerable projects, if the school program is open and flexible.

TEENAGE TENANT TRAINING COUNCIL (3T's)
NEW YORK CITY

The deterioration of city housing can have an almost devastating impact on the lives of those who live in the inner city. In nearly all cities there are areas where dwellings are littered, rat-infested, and structurally unsound.

Take New York City's Chelsea section, for example. It is an old, flat part of the city where, when the wind blows, litter flies up in the faces of pedestrians. Its decaying tenements are now heavily populated by Spanish-speaking people whose language problems often make it difficult for them to determine their rights and to voice their complaints to the appropriate authority.

In 1966 a number of adult residents met with a small group of neighborhood youths and members of the staff of the Hudson Guild Community Center to discuss what could be done about housing in Chelsea. They decided to establish the Teenage Tenant Training Council, known as the 3T's and designed to provide help on housing problems. The idea was to employ neighborhood youths during summers to uncover and report housing code violations, to insure that landlords were not overcharging tenants, and to organize tenants' associations so that they themselves could deal with their landlords.

The first director of the Teenage Tenant Training Council

was an educator from New York City's public schools who had worked with the Hudson Guild's summer program. It was he who initiated the meeting at which the decision was made to set up the 3T's; he also wrote the proposal for the program and got it approved and funded.

A little later another educator took over as director of the Council. His chief responsibility was to work with the enrollees, fifteen- to eighteen-year-old boys, and to train them for the work they were to do. He was so successful in his training program that, after five years, he was able to turn over the reins to a young man who had worked with the Council since it was first formed.

The structure of the 3T's continues to be almost the same as when it was founded. The program is supervised by a paid director and two young assistants and has the aid of a secretary. The young people do most of the program's leg-work, and in group sessions with the director, they make most of the program's important decisions.

All the enrollees are paid workers from the Neighborhood Youth Corps, a program of the federal government. Unfortunately, New York City has suffered budget cutbacks so the number of slots assigned to the 3T's has fallen to twenty; at one time there were as many as forty young people working in the program. However, the budget for the program has always been very small.

One of the great strengths of the program has been the continuity of its youthful personnel. Each summer seventy-five percent of the boys from the previous summer return to work. By the time these boys have had two or three years of experience, they are as competent as most adults would be at handling the complex tasks of getting landlords to make the repairs that will bring their tenements up to acceptable standards.

A young man who is registered with the Neighborhood Youth Corps and wants to enroll in the 3T's simply goes to its office in the Hudson Guild Community Center and applies. Unfortunately, his chances of being accepted are slim because there may be fifty or more applicants for the five to ten slots open each year. After he applies, he is interviewed by a number of program members and the director; they then make the decision on admission. Few questions are asked about background, since prior delinquency is not a consideration. The sole criterion for acceptance or rejection is what the director likes to call "heart"—a quality to be found in a true and fierce desire to work in the program. Only those who seem to have this quality are selected. The program has thus far been made available only to boys, because the members believe that entering unfamiliar tenement buildings in the neighborhood would be physically dangerous for girls.

A boy who has been accepted completes a ten-day instructional program before he goes on the Neighborhood Youth Corps payroll. They are instructed in the details of the housing code and learn the general rule that any health hazard is a code violation. They also learn about rent-paying and rent-withholding procedures, the method for reporting violations, and the way to approach tenants about fighting housing violations. This last aspect of the training is particularly important since many tenants in the neighborhood are unaware of their rights and fearful of protest, and since many of the newly-enrolled youths are emotionally immature and have had little experience in dealing with adults. Role-playing is a major part of the orientation; veterans of the program simulate suspicious or intimidated tenants and the new enrollees try to create rapport. Another important part of the training is instruction about their rights in terms of the landlords and superintendents who frequently harass 3T workers.

After completing the instructional program, a youth is assigned to one of four crews, each of which has responsibility for one-fourth of Chelsea. He is assigned to work with one other boy. The director makes these assignments and makes

sure there is at least one Spanish-speaking boy on each team
—a necessity if the team is to be effective in Chelsea. The
youth then begins his regular work; he puts in five seven-hour
days per week, plus two evenings, part of which time he
volunteers.

Under the direction of his crew's leaders, the youth helps
survey the neighborhood to which he is assigned, looking for
trash in vacant lots, broken glass, smashed-in doors on vacant
buildings, and other signs of disrepair. His crew then prepares
a detailed report, which may be submitted to the city's Housing Inspection Authority for action.

Next the crew selects one building in its area for thorough
inspection. As soon as this is completed, preparation for the
inspection of another is begun. Three days advance notice of
the inspection is given to tenants but *not* to superintendents
or landlords who might use the time to work against the inspection. Teams are then given identification badges and
complaint forms, and on the assigned day each team attempts
to inspect its share of the building's apartments. The workers
knock on doors, show their identification cards, and explain
that they have come to check for housing violations. They add
that their purpose is to make sure that the landlord corrects
violations and they advise the tenants that if violations are
not corrected, the Rent Control Board can force the landlord
to reduce the rent. If there is only one person in the flat, one
teammate explains the purpose of the inspection while the
other scans the premises for violations. If more than one
person is at home, every effort is made to conduct separate
interviews with each one; this seems to yield better results.
With the consent of the tenants, the team makes a list of violations they find and asks the tenants to make a list of the
violations *they* see. The two lists are compared, and the tenant
is then asked to sign a complaint form if there are violations.
The young people feel this procedure helps tenants to identify
violations. The teams bring the forms back to headquarters,

and the 3T's write to the landlord requesting that the violations be corrected. If this produces no response, the Housing Authority is asked to take action. Many landlords have been prosecuted for failing to comply.

In addition to pushing to correct code violations, 3T youths perform at least two other important functions for the tenants of Chelsea. Through education and intervention, they attempt to stop unscrupulous landlords from cheating uncomprehending Spanish-speaking tenants by the use of such devices as juggling rent receipts. They also attempt to help tenants help themselves by organizing tenant associations to pressure landlords into fulfilling their obligations. Four or five associations have usually been organized each summer. Unfortunately these associations tend to fall apart in September when 3T participants leave the program. Furthermore, landlords often realize that if they can stall action until September, they can probably escape making repairs. For these reasons, the Hudson Guild has been flooded with requests that the 3T's become a year-round program. Unfortunately this is unlikely because there are not enough funds.

Landlords and superintendents still cause trouble for 3T youths and frequently call the police to keep them away from their buildings. But cooperation from tenants and other neighborhood people, combined with a little youthful guile, usually overcome opposition. Chelsea residents were initially a little suspicious and skeptical of these boys who claimed they could do something to improve neighborhood housing. But these feelings have vanished. The residents see now that the 3T's are serious and back up their claims. Moreover, they have seen how the program has taken numbers of youths off the streets in the summer and given them useful jobs. As for the boys themselves, the rewards of the program have come partly from their Neighborhood Youth Corps salaries but more substantially from the confidence and the knowledge they have gained about accepting real responsibility. The fact that a veteran of the program's ranks is now taking over the director's post from a civil servant of long years' experience is ample testimony to the success of the program in this regard.

Those who wish to consider using the Teenage Tenant Training Council as a model to be adapted to their own community housing problems might think about the possibility of making their project a part of the school curriculum, with course credit being given to participants. It might be possible, for example, to include such a project in the social studies curriculum and make the work young people do in the community an experiential component of the school program.

DADE COUNTY YOUTH COUNCIL
DADE COUNTY, FLORIDA

The two projects that have just been described—EARTH and the Teenage Tenant Training Council—each attack a single community problem. In Dade County, Florida, where the metropolitan government covers all Miami, Miami Beach, and the surrounding area, a somewhat different approach to involving students in community problem-solving seemed to be necessary; the Dade County Youth Council grew out of this need.

The formal organization of the Council stemmed from the ideas and objectives generated at a three-day "lock-in" held in October 1970. Students representing high schools from all over Dade County met in lengthy workshop sessions proposing and debating solutions to problems in seven major areas: drug abuse, government policies and politics, services to urban areas, services to migrants, environmental pollution, intergroup relations, and juvenile delinquency. This "lock-in" was sponsored by the National Conference of Christians and Jews, the Dade County public schools, and the United Fund.

It received widespread publicity in Dade County and led to the action program of the Youth Council.

The Youth Council was organized early in 1971* when clubs from various area schools began holding meetings to discuss common problems. But the Council was not actually perceived as an important body until the Florida region of the National Conference of Christians and Jews won for it from ESEA Title IV a fairly large annual grant, which allowed the Council to sponsor various kinds of meetings and to develop a program. Some time later the United Fund of Dade County joined the National Conference of Christians and Jews as cosponsor of the Youth Council. Their work was, for the most part, limited to making adult contacts for the Council and to obtaining funds and services. It was the young people themselves, operating with a minimum of adult supervision, who developed and carried on a varied program of community-related activities.

The Dade County Youth Council attempted to give area youth a voice in handling all the major problems that affected them. In a sense it expanded on the old idea of representative student government, which has traditionally been confined to schools and limited to the problems of the school. The Youth Council was outward-looking and dedicated to working on problems that confronted the entire metropolitan community.

The Youth Council was structured to serve its main goal of representing all Dade County's youth at all levels of official decision-making that affected their lives. Each of the forty public and parochial high schools in the county elected six representatives to the Youth Council. In addition, any

---

* The Council has since been dissolved in favor of another program that involves young people in still different ways. The United Fund Youth Program involves high school students in planning and policy-making that affect social services, youth services, and other supportive services provided to the citizens of Dade County. Young people also participate in various projects of the Volunteer Action Center.

high school student in Dade County could be a member of the Council, and at one time there were approximately four hundred and eighty members. Each member belonged to one of the Council's five task forces: Government Policy and Politics, Drug Abuse, Services to Migrants, Services to Urban Areas, and Intergroup Relations.

It was within these task forces that the bulk of the Youth Council's real work was done. Each task force held a general meeting twice a month, but these meetings did not begin to reflect the amount of work actually done. For example, during one of his task force's active periods, a student might have worked for more than thirty hours a week after school and on weekends.

In addition to the task forces, the Youth Council had a legislative arm, the Youth Commission. The Commission's organizational structure sought to replicate Dade County's governing body, the Dade County Commission. The Youth Commission drafted proposals for laws and ordinances, based on ideas contributed either by the task forces or by the Youth Commissioners themselves, and provided the Youth Council with concrete bills to present to the County Commission. The members of the Youth Commission were elected to their positions by the Council's voting members. The voting members were students chosen by their respective schools to belong to the Council, as opposed to those who joined the Council of their own volition. Finally, the Youth Council had an Executive Board, elected by the voting members and composed of the heads of each task force, the Youth Commissioners, and the president, vice-president, and secretary of the entire Youth Council. The Executive Board made the decisions that affected the Council as a whole, deciding, for example, what Youth Commission work the Youth Council should recommend to the Dade County Commission for action or approval.

Although the Council had a carefully defined structure, it was informal in operation. The informality resulted primarily from the fact that any Dade County high school student could join the Council. It came also from the open door policy of the Council's presiding officers—a policy that emphasized that Council members were always available to discuss any problem or idea a member might suggest. The Council later worked out a scheme to make itself even more flexible and open; any Council members who felt they would like to express a minority opinion could form a caucus and publicize their views as the opinion of a Youth Council Caucus. One of the things that the Dade County Youth Council was anxious to prove was that "youth" does not represent a single point of view, as many think, but that youth, like the adult community, is filled with lively, democratic disagreement. No Council opinion or position was ever presented as the unanimous opinion of youth or of the Council, unless this was actually the case, and minority views were regularly given fair and ample treatment. As one president of the Youth Council said: "The Youth Council came into being because youths in general felt that doors were not open to them; we want to be careful not to shut our doors on anybody else."

The concrete accomplishments of the Youth Council were many and varied. The Government Policy and Politics task force organized a nonpartisan drive to get out the eighteen-year-old vote. This drive included a program of voter education. The same task force, with the help of Miami community leaders, acted as intermediaries between young demonstrators at the 1972 Democratic National Convention and the Miami police by working to develop understanding between the two groups and to avoid violence. The Intergroup Relations task force operated a series of tri-racial opinion exchanges in which students from predominantly white Miami Beach Senior High, predominantly black Jackson High and predominantly Latin Miami Senior High met together to discuss "racial problems, mix-ups, and hang-ups." The Services to Migrants and the Services to Urban Areas task forces joined together to conduct a tutorial program for children of seasonal farm workers in the south Dade County area.

The Youth Commission drafted a restructuring of the Dade County Drug Abuse Advisory Board, a reorganization of Dade County's summer job program for youths, new laws regarding school buses and mini-bikes, and a report on the progress of Dade County school desegregation. Legislation very similar to what the Commission proposed regarding mini-bikes was adopted. One of the Youth Council's proudest achievements was introducing youth representatives into the highest levels of Dade County government; by the end of 1972 there was at least one youth (nonvoting) on every County board. The Council also spent much time and money trying to organize youth on a national level through such activities as conferences and communications centers. These were only a few of the many activities.

One thing the Council's officers were particularly hopeful about was the possibility that some day the Council's activities would mesh with the Dade County school curriculum. They hoped that the kinds of things they were doing to help solve some of the community's problems might become the experiential component of, for example, their study of American government.

Many of the Dade County Youth Council's structural elements recommend it as a model for youth in other cities who feel that a large-scale general representative body would serve their needs. Chief among these elements were the Council's flexibility and independence.

OTHER PROGRAMS

The programs just described suggest some of the ways in which students can serve as community problem-solvers. But the range of possibilities is really unlimited, and schools that would like to help students become active in community problem-solving may find further suggestions in the following brief descriptions of other projects:

☐ The Berkeley (California) Youth Council is an interesting variation on the Dade County project. It has some of the same organizational features as the Dade County Youth Council—a slate of elected officers and most of its work done through committees. But its operating procedures are even more flexible than Dade Council's were, and its possibilities for modifying its emphasis from time to time are perhaps greater. The Berkeley Council, which was founded in 1966 by three individuals—the student body president at Berkeley High School, a senior at a Catholic girls' school, and a member of the hippie community—has continued to maintain a high degree of diversity. It has an office in Berkeley's City Hall.

Among the Berkeley Council's concrete achievements have been the publication of a pamphlet dealing with employment opportunities in the Berkeley area and one dealing with the relationship between young people and the law; the drafting of recommendations regarding Berkeley's school integration plan; and the mediation of conflicts arising from confrontations between youth and city authorities.

☐ The Student Board of Education of Santa Barbara, California, is a somewhat more structured version of the Dade and Berkeley Councils. Students in each Santa Barbara high school elect representatives to the Student Board. The Board holds regular public meetings and makes proposals to the Santa Barbara School Board based on ideas developed at its meetings and the surveys it conducts of the Santa Barbara student population. The purpose of the Student Board is twofold: (1) to provide a channel for Santa Barbara students to bring matters of student concern to the attention of the city's adult school board, and (2) to give students an increased awareness of the instructional and fiscal problems that public education faces. Among the Student Board proposals accepted by the adult board are the inclusion of students on curriculum advisory committees, the devotion of one school day each term to the study of the deterioration of the environment, and the establishment of a committee appointed by the Student Board to rule upon student dress and grooming codes.

☐ Students Teaching Our Public (STOP) was the ildea of a senior studying consumer economics at Patrick Henry High School in San Diego, California. Students participating in the project set up a consumer information booth at the local shopping center and named it CEPA for Consumer Economists for Public Awareness. The booth is manned by students for one hour each day during the peak shopping period, and shoppers can come there with their questions. Other students solicit queries by scouting the center and talking with shoppers. Each shopper who has a consumer problem or question is invited to go to the CEPA booth, write out his question, put his mailing address on an envelope provided him and leave the cost of postage.

At the end of the hour, the questions are brought back to the school, and students begin to research the problems in their consumer education class. Talking among themselves and with their teacher, they try to come up with answers to questions and solutions to problems. If they find that they do not have the information needed, they call the Consumer Affairs Department on the phone and ask the official responsible for help. In their search for relevant information and for solutions to problems they have been in touch with such groups as the Association of Supermarket Managers, the Poultry Association, the Vegetable Growers Association, and many others.

After a specific question has been carefully researched, the pertinent information is written up and mailed to the concerned consumer.

☐ The Morrisania Community Center Lead Poisoning Program was formed to deal with the problem of lead poisoning in children. Lead poisoning usually results from eating chips of paint that fall from old walls and decaying woodwork and is a terrible yet still relatively unexplored plague of slum areas. It attacks its victims slowly, taking months or more for the poison to accumulate and be identified. Its ultimate effects are mental retardation and sometimes death. A few years ago it was estimated that more than seven percent of the young children living in New York's South Bronx section were afflicted to some degree.

The Student Health Organization of the Einstein Medical College, working through the Morrisania Community Center, hires neighborhood teenagers to find afflicted children in various South Bronx neighborhoods. During the summer of 1970, for example, one hundred and ten neighborhood young people put on medical jackets and tested more than three thousand children.

The program now continues through the school year. The young people first survey a neighborhood to find out which apartments have children in them. They then take the children's medical histories and make appointments for a doctor to come to take blood tests. On the appointed day they return with a doctor, clean one apartment to prepare it for use as a testing center, gather up the children, and hold them one-by-one while the doctor takes the blood samples. They then take the blood samples to a laboratory for analysis, keeping complete records of all the samples. When abnormally high amounts of lead in their blood are found, the young people return to the homes of these children to arrange for further tests and treatment.

☐ The Legal Representatives Project of the New York Youth Services Agency dealt with another problem that recurs with unfortunate frequency in many urban areas—youth in trouble with the law. Workers on this project attempted to bring about a healthy and relatively frictionless relationship between the youth of ghetto areas and the legal system. If a young man who was enrolled in a branch of the YSA's Satellite Program got into trouble, he could contact one of fourteen youths who were affiliated with the Satellite Program and who were known as legal representatives.

The legal representative began by screening cases. He checked, for example, to make sure that the youth in trouble was actually enrolled in the Satellite Program. He then contracted the YSA attorney and, following his instructions, explained to the youth what the attorney had said about his situation. He also made sure that the youth was appropriately dressed when he reported for his hearing. If the case warranted it, the legal representative worked with the boy's parents and neighbors, informing them of his predicament and occasionally marshalling support for him. The representatives also helped the YSA attorneys in investigations and appeared in court with affidavits and motions for adjournment.

Many of the legal representatives themselves had histories of legal violations, but this was not the reason for their selection. They were chosen because of their deep commitment to ghetto youth.

☐ Action Community was an experimental program originated by a biology teacher in the Detroit schools and sponsored by the Detroit School Board. Thirty students from three Detroit inner city high schools were involved in a project to identify problems within their schools and communities and to undertake activities that might offer a solution to these problems. The project was developed as a noncredit course, but students were released from regular classroom study while they worked on the problems. The project was located in a local church where the thirty teenagers met with a staff of three teachers.

The first semester was spent identifying community problems. The teenagers scouted their neighborhoods with instamatic cameras to capture on film evidence of unsanitary conditions, unsafe housing, poor recreational facilities, youth unemployment, air and water pollution, and many other problems. During this fact-finding period, students took bus trips outside their neighborhood to visit industrial complexes, low income housing areas, and neighborhoods having high crime rates. On these group trips the teenagers interviewed community residents to obtain their perceptions of their problems.

In the next phase of the program—the problem-solving phase—the students selected the specific problems on which to focus. After much discussion, the thirty students divided into three interest groups: housing, youth unemployment, and recreation. Each group decided to use problem-solving methods to deal with its particular interest. This meant defining the problem, identifying and analyzing alternative solutions, choosing the most rational and feasible alternative, designing a plan of action, implementing the plan, and then evaluating what had been done.

Stated briefly, the solutions arrived at after careful study were these: (1) the housing group prepared a slide presentation to be used with various community groups to show what loans and grants are available to low-income citizens for rehabilitating their homes, (2) the youth unemployment group took action to help develop, at one of the participating high schools, a work-study program that would give high school youths some opportunities to gain job experience, (3) the recreation group planned and took action to help the community develop an enlarged recreational area on a vacant lot owned by an industrial firm.

The program chairman reported that the teachers who worked with this project shared the hope that one outcome of student participation would be an improvement in self-concept as the teenagers gained confidence in their ability to meet, talk with, and work with adults in their own and nearby communities. The report describing the project contains the following statement:

We feel that . . . we have succeeded with some of our basic objectives of (*1*) providing real life experiences with relevant environmental problems, thereby increasing the confidence of at least a few youth to even speak to administrators and seriously consider becoming involved in constructive community action in the future, (*2*) "reaching" some of these youth at a real "feeling" level in an environment which was otherwise filled with adults threatening their freedom and smothering them with preconceived notions of how they should act, and (*3*) increased awareness of issues associated with each of their project areas—housing, unemployment, and recreation.

☐ The Young World Development Program is a youth component of the American Freedom from Hunger Foundation and seeks to arouse national public awareness of the causes and extent of worldwide hunger and poverty. Young World Development has organized more than two hundred "Walks for Development" all over the country. Some five hundred thousand youths have hiked twenty to thirty miles each to bring attention to poverty and hunger and to raise money to fight them. These walks have already raised more than $11,000,000. Most of the Young World Development coordinators are young people; they range in age from twelve to twenty but mainly encompass high school juniors to college sophomores. They set up their own offices when a walk is planned, contact the proper local officials, make speeches, print posters, win endorsements, distribute brochures, and recruit walkers.

A FURTHER WORD

The programs described in this chapter, and other programs that involve young people in community problem-solving, strongly suggest that the possibilities are enormous for schools that wish to engage their students in the problem-solving process. Moreover, what schools need to do to activate such programs is in most cases neither extraordinarily difficult nor prohibitively expensive. Many, many students are eager for such programs; their dedication and enthusiasm are better insurance for success than extensive adult supervision or large sums of money. In fact, according to people who have worked with or observed many of the various projects, the programs that seem to be particularly successful are often those where the school's commitment, in terms of both supervision and money, is limited—limited either deliberately or by force of circumstance.

But there are two very important elements that schools sponsoring community problem-solving programs should try to supply: (1) a visible and genuine belief in the sincerity and the ability of youthful participants, and (2) training programs adequate to the tasks that young people will eventually undertake by themselves. With this kind of support, young people move ahead with enthusiasm and efficiency to help deal with the problems their communities face.

YOUTH
as communicators

THE LUNCHROOM POETS

Straight after sixth
straight down to the lunchroom
come & watch the poets.

Imaginations flying everywhere
upwards
    downwards
flying higher & still higher.

Poets in every corner
smiling
listening
inspired by every sound around.

Fingers bubbling with new words
on every line
writing
jotting . . . scribbling
all feelings of the youth.

The youth
the young
the high school kids
come & watch them
describe the world around us.

Karen Schnorr[1]

1. From "A Grave for My Eyes," Supplement, *Teachers and Writers Collaborative Newsletter* (c/o Public School Number 3, 490 Hudson Street, New York, New York 10004).

For young people, one of the most significant facets of growing up is discovering the need for communicating and finding ways to satisfy it. Many of today's youth are demonstrating their awareness of the need for communication and their often unique ability to use all available media in their efforts to satisfy this need.

Through his efforts to communicate each young person is also examining himself, his peers, his adult associates, his world; he is contemplating his concerns and trying to come to terms with them.

School, which is one place for communicating, provides an important forum for raising questions, testing assumptions, arriving at conclusions, and evaluating conclusions. It is in the school, too, that students find many of the necessary tools for communicating—typewriters, tape recorders, cameras, teleprinters, videotape machines, radio and television receivers, art materials, construction materials, and many other useful resources.

With the school as a major base, other avenues of communication frequently become available—radio and television outlets in the community, newspapers and magazines, and an increasing number of art forms. Community readiness to make its communications resources—including personnel —available to young people is reflected in many of the activities described in this chapter.

NEWSPAPERS

QUEENS AND HARLEM, NEW YORK

Students and teachers alike have long been involved in various types of student publications, but most efforts have been school based, depending entirely on school resources, making few demands upon the community, and turning out products that had little or no specific value for the community. But new precedents have been set in successful and continuing student publications that demonstrate the possibilities of expanding beyond the school.

In 1968 the *New York Times* conducted discussions with community representatives in several ghetto areas to determine where and with whom a newspaper project could take root. Two areas were chosen—Corona-Elmhurst in Queens and Harlem in Manhattan. Several young people in these areas showed interest in the proposed *Times'* projects, and the *Corona-East Elmhurst Transition Press* and *Black Spectrum* (initially called *Harlem Youth Speaks*) were born. The hope of the young people was that their newspapers could serve as an instrument for change by reflecting their community's needs, frustrations, and aspirations.

These papers are supported by an annual grant made available by the New York Times Foundation and divided equally between the two papers. This grant provides enough to pay small salaries to the student staff and covers the costs of newsprint, printing, and incidental expenses.

The *Transition Press*, begun in 1969, is based at the local library. The number of editorial staff members ranges from five to nine and is composed mostly of high school seniors. At least two members of the staff have been with the paper since its inception and are developing professional skills. While the inevitable large staff turnover creates some production difficulties, it also creates opportunities for more students to participate. The staff participates in everything except the actual printing of the paper, which is handled by a local printer.

The staff is encouraged to come up with ideas for their own stories. These ideas are presented to other staff members who offer their opinions on what angle to take, possible sources of data, how best to handle the interview if there is to be one, and whether the story merits a picture. Two reporters from the *New York Times* work with the staff, and one of them meets with the young workers each Saturday throughout the year. The discussion is informal with the *Times* reporter usually participating only when asked directly by a young staffer. Stories are assigned and deadlines are set. Responsibilities are shared among the students, and duties are assigned according to experience. Most jobs, including copyreading, assigning stories, and writing headlines, editorials, columns, and book reviews, are undertaken on a rotation basis.

Staff members read and compare coverage of a particular story by the major metropolitan papers, and they look critically at their own stories to determine whether they have reported fairly and objectively. This process enables the *Times* reporters to give their young colleagues a firm grounding in professional skills.

Since the priority of the *Times* is to teach techniques, the staff is not pressured to publish on a regular basis. To the delight of the staff, however, community interest in the paper, usually published bimonthly, is definitely growing. This is indicated, in part, by the growing volume of letters to the editor. On one occasion the community actually saved the paper when, in the face of economic losses, the *New York Times* began to have second thoughts about continuing to underwrite the *Transition Press*. A petition signed by eighteen hundred Corona-East Elmhurst residents convinced the *Times* that the paper was indeed performing a vital function.

Several important facts emerged from this petition and from the letters sent to the *Times* by individuals and groups:

☐ The community needed a paper and would continue to support the *Transition Press*.

☐ The staff of the *Press* had acquired the reporting and production skills necessary to fill the need and gain the respect of the community.

☐ The paper was trusted as a vehicle for information, dissent, and entertainment.

☐ The community regarded the paper as a unifying factor for a diverse citizenry.

Black Spectrum, the *Times*' other inner city venture, has had similar success. In one progress report the *Times* reporter in charge of the project noted the dedication of the student staff: "The young people have been marvelous. There have been five or six stick-with-it people who have attended almost every session and who have taken the lead and the responsibility."

Since the project began in 1970, the editorial staff has increased to ten, nine of whom were high school students at the time they joined the staff. Initially the small incentive payments offered by the *Times* tempted some young people to drop in to collect their money and then drop out again. Now, to be paid, regular attendance and regular input are mandatory. This was decided by the young people themselves.

Black Spectrum is put together entirely by young people throughout the year. The staff meets weekly with a *Times* staff copy editor at Columbia University's Graduate School of Journalism where they have the use of its facilities.

Like the *Transition Press*, this paper illustrates an interesting and imaginative use of a resource for implementing change. *Black Spectrum* is more consciously militant, more politically oriented, and contains more opinion than its Corona counterpart. Editorializing and factual reporting often appear on the same page, with no clear demarcation. The paper contains little objective reporting, but it does reflect the spirit, the quality, and the flavor of the community. For example, messages like "Freedom Comes Through Struggle!" "The Agents Must Be Weeded Out and Eliminated," and "Power to the Marksman!" reflect the militant feelings prevalent in the area. There have been repeated exhortations to honor the memory of the Soledad Three, and there was strong support for the release of Angela Davis. However, with the passage of time, the writing has become more professional and the point of view more moderate.

Taking the stand that publicity is the only way to get action, the paper has concerned itself with sanitation, the mishandling of monies by anti-poverty agencies, the drug problem, and other issues. *Black Spectrum* is concerned with the quality of life of black Americans, both for the present and for the future, and it is deeply rooted in the Harlem community.

HIGH SCHOOL STUDENT INFORMATION CENTER
WASHINGTON, D.C.

In contrast to *Transition Press* and *Black Spectrum*, which are well established and devoted to their respective communities, the High School Student Information Center (SIC), located in Washington, D.C., is addressed to high school students anywhere in the nation.

SIC is the brainchild of four high school juniors who lived in Maryland but were within commuting distance of Washington. These young people felt that schools did not operate in their interest, and they believed that many other high school students shared this feeling. They decided, therefore, that they would like to provide appropriate services to young people who wanted to make changes in their schools.

The students' first plan, in 1970, was to establish a national network of information centers in many cities. They realized that this would be very expensive and so, prior to writing a proposal applying for grant funds, they sought advice. They went to the Stern Family Fund, talked to the executive director, and secured a planning grant.

The scheme devised by the students was very detailed and unrealistically optimistic. It involved, first, the selection of twenty-five major cities, a major suburb of each of these cities, and twenty-five rural areas. From each of these sites the students proposed to collect data concerning socio-economic groupings, organizational activities, power structures, and publications. A student representative would be selected from each school to act as the information link between that school and SIC. These representatives would report all events to the Center and would be responsible for publicizing SIC in their particular school. The writers of the proposal requested $60,000 to finance the project, earmarking $35,000 to employ five regular staff members and thirty young consultants and $25,000 for travel and for publications. After the report had been read and commented on by school administrators, youth coordinators, and student groups, the writers of the proposal took their document to the Board of Directors of the Stern Family Fund. The proposal was not exactly "shot down," one student recalls ruefully, "but I guess there must have been a lot of raised eyebrows at the kind of money we were asking for . . . Anyway they gave us $20,000."

The project required drastic revision at this point, but SIC decided to concentrate on gathering information as a basis for the project. With a staff of ten, they began to collect information about federal and state education legislation, including guidelines, HEW programs, and statements concerning youth; state school board policies regarding high school students; theories of alternative school systems; and change-oriented programs initiated by high school students. They also collected copies of high school underground papers and newspapers concerned with educational reform. In addition, correspondence was initiated with lawyers, educators, students, and other individuals involved in educational change.

The group also began working with two student news services that had already been in existence for over a year. One of these operated a high school underground newspaper exchange, and largely because SIC students worked closely with it, the number of publications included in the exchange increased from forty to seventy-eight. SIC also worked with an information agency serving high school underground publications. It revamped their newsletter, changing both content and format, and undertook the financing and publication of ten fortnightly issues.

Information gathered during the digging period was checked for accuracy and put into packets. SIC then directed its attention to the regular publication of its own *High School Student Information Center Newsletter*.[2] Contacts established during the initial period were approached again for fresh information. High school mailing lists were consulted, and letters were written requesting information about interesting new developments.

The three main facets of the SIC operation have become (*1*) collection, (*2*) compilation, and (*3*) dissemination of information. The information gathered is prepared for distribution by members of the staff or by people hired by the staff. Copies are mailed to high school students, high school underground newspapers, educational officials, educators, youth coordinators, and high school organizers such as adults in organizations such as the American Civil Liberties Union who help high school students develop papers and advise them of their rights as students.

SIC sometimes hires high school students for specific assignments. For example, a Denver student was hired to write about having her illegitimate baby in a maternity home and putting it up for adoption. Another student described her experiences in an alternative school.

The Student Information Center began operating in 1970. Since that time publications have appeared periodically. The main concern is with putting out a positive, useful, and informative product. Technically it is not a highly professional effort, and good writing, accurate spelling, and grammatical construction are sometimes sacrificed. But importantly, the staff is aware of the strengths and weaknesses of its system of operation and remains confident that valid ways to institute change do exist. This editorial exchange with a reader illustrates the magazine's philosophy:

---

2. Available from SIC, 1010 Wisconsin Avenue N.W., Washington, D. C. 20007.

To the Editor:

There will be feints, twists, dodges, and the facade of response but don't you ever believe that a high school principal or a board of education, or a school superintendent is going to give you the power to run your own life. . . .

SIC response:

. . . We agree on the facts about education, jobs, college, etc. but not on how to deal with these facts. To make it possible for high school students to have choices about what happens to them in their *present* we don't believe we can ignore the system that has taught them what their choices supposedly are. . . .

The desire to work within the system to change the system is the crux of editorial thinking at SIC. The focus is on solid and complete information, geared to student needs and interests and ranging from information on birth control, the draft, and curriculum innovations to an article on the dangers of the hot dog.

THE CITY ARTS WORKSHOP
NEW YORK CITY

The visual and literary arts offer young people another way to communicate with their community and their peers and serve as a means to press for constructive political and social change. Like the newspaper projects, many experiments in the arts are based upon forming a close relationship between a working professional and a young person. Such approaches result in a product that can be seen, responded to, and claimed as one's own.

City Arts Workshop, Inc., (CAW) was founded by three young artists, one of whom had worked with the New York City Department of Cultural Affairs. CAW receives funds from individual contributions and small grants from foundations. In spite of constant funding problems, CAW has established a unique and dramatic form of creative communication firmly rooted in community life—murals, sculpture, and mosaics.

Before developing a project for working with young people, CAW's founders asked themselves some important questions: Can people who are not necessarily "artists" express themselves graphically? Can they make a visual statement about themselves as individuals or as part of a group, or a movement, or a widely held belief? Can they leave upon the steel and concrete of the city an imprint of themselves? By making a public and dramatic visual statement, do their self-concepts become clearer? Is their sense of common identity sharpened? Is it worthwhile or necessary to say anything at all? The group felt that the answer to each of these questions was "yes."

Since the time it was founded in 1968, the Workshop's operations have extended into schools and parks and hallways—with significant results. "People just can't believe . . . that their hands can influence anything in this city at all. They are surprised and gratified when they find they can," says the Workshop's director.

All kinds of people, mostly young minority groups from depressed neighborhoods, have found that they *can* create and that they *can* have influence. CAW uses simple approaches. An obvious talent in drawing or painting is not a prerequisite, and many participants had not had any art experience before they executed their first design with the CAW staff. The materials used are simple and easy to obtain—paint, cement, glass, paper, and wood. Equipment is also simple—cameras, projectors, and wooden moulds. Add the informality of the workshop to the ease of production, and it is easy to see why CAW has elicited such an enthusiastic response.

Teenagers and younger children play focal roles and assume major responsibilities in CAW's various ventures. For example, in the production workshop, approximately two dozen participants, directed by a staff artist, plan and execute large exterior wall murals for their community with the young workshop members involved in all stages of development. First the teenagers discuss the issues most central to their lives and select a theme. At this stage, many participants begin to express doubts—doubts mainly stemming from their lack of art training. The staff artist tries to instill confidence by, for example, asking new members to act out their concepts while other members take polaroid photographs of these dramatizations. The photographs are then studied critically, and their relative merits discussed.

Next a mock-up is begun, and a scaled-down version of the intended wall is simulated. Workshop members use it as a backdrop to experiment with positioning the polaroid pictures and arranging them in different designs. This stage of the project provides an opportunity to develop an aesthetic sense as well as to develop the give and take necessary to the group process. When the final layout for the wall is decided upon, the photographs are placed in an opaque projector to magnify and project them, the design units are sketched in the desired proportions, and they are painted on outdoor plywood panels, which are installed by professionals. More recently workshop members have been painting directly on outside walls.

In CAW's first project, in the summer of 1968, a group of teenagers helped residents of a housing project in Manhattan's Lower East Side create a mural in sandcast cement for their recreation center. The ease and informality of the workshop and its open air location attracted even dubious older community members and a total of one hundred persons participated in the project.

"Following the successful completion of this project," recalls the director, "we felt that we wanted to maintain contact with the teenagers of this neighborhood whose lives are rooted in the violence of the street and whose greatest challenge is to survive. To do this we realized we had to upstage the streets and propose alternatives which were equally dramatic."

CAW therefore suggested to twelve neighborhood boys that they organize a workshop to create a mural in vivid hues on a prominently located wall. CAW staff artists trained the boys in mural techniques. Then with staff support, the boys went out into the neighborhood to get suggestions for a motif and to get reactions to their own ideas. Ultimately the mural motif was decided upon. The result of their efforts is indeed compelling. Larger than lifesize red and blue backgrounds illustrate such aspects of community life as drug abuse, fist fights, gang wars, and police payoffs. The mural, which is fifty-five feet by twenty-six feet, was developed from left to right with the last sequence depicting a young male figure, twenty-six feet high, turning his back on negativism with his fist clenched in the black power salute. This focal figure depicted not violence and destruction but hope, a feeling that outsiders often do not associate with street youth.

Two more projects were undertaken by this group of teenagers. The boys' workshop completed a major mural about black liberation and are now trying to get the New York City administration to fulfill its original commitment to mount it on a huge wall overlooking the Franklin D. Roosevelt Drive. The teenage girls' workshop, determined not to be outdone, executed a one hundred and thirty-two-foot painting that occupies two continuous walls and represents the black woman in America.

Not content to work only in public areas, the teenage workshops tried to make themselves available for other projects in the community. Workshop members met with residents in area housing projects and encouraged them to work on small-scale murals in the hallways of their apartment buildings. Many such projects have been completed, and others are being planned.

The City Art Workshop's most ambitious project has been

Part of a brilliantly colored mural covering the side of a block-long building in New York's Lower East Side.   CITY ARTS
WORKSHOP

the creation of Patchwork Plaza in Washington Square Park in Greenwich Village. Stretching about forty feet in diameter, it is made up of seven hundred equilateral triangles cast in cement. The surface of each large triangle is covered with mosaic designs created by the Greenwich Village community, which the workshop sought to bring together. Symbols of the occult mingle with revolutionary and peace symbols, signature plates, and a memorial to Attica. An important by-product of the construction process itself was that it brought together people who would not otherwise have met and come to know each other. Passers-by were intrigued at the sight of a bunch of kids sitting on the ground in the park pasting colored glass tiles on triangular pieces of brown paper as a first stage of the process. Mothers wheeling baby carriages stopped to ask questions and sometimes lent a hand. Old men sunning themselves on the park benches would sometimes stick the tiles to the triangles; next day they would often stroll over to offer suggestions on the later stages.

CAW culminates its efforts with what the youth like to call "festivals." Project participants and other members of the community come together to celebrate the completion of their projects. The work is formally unveiled, and people mingle and talk together. Other community groups have used these occasions to approach CAW for help on community projects in their respective areas.

Conducting leadership training workshops is another important function of CAW. Fifteen teenagers, who have already worked on a mural or painting and who have shown interest and determination in creating, organizing, and implementing projects, are chosen to participate in the training sessions, which are held every day during the summer and two or three days a week during the school year. These teenagers, working under the supervision of a staff artist, are given guidelines on how to direct and run a workshop. They are then assigned to help out with projects when requests from communities are received, and they receive a fee for the services they perform. Making the murals, therefore, becomes a kind of job, and the individual's degree of dedication, responsibility, and proficiency helps determine the number of his assignments and the extent of his monetary reward. The young staff assistant is gradually given the practical experience necessary to run an entire workshop if he chooses to do so in the future.

Young graduates of the leadership workshops have faced a variety of challenges over the last two years. One, for example, arose when Manhattan's Park East High School asked CAW's help on a mural that its students wanted to make. CAW chose two sixteen-year-old staff assistants, graduates of the production and leadership workshops, to initiate and run the workshop at Park East entirely on their own initiative, with a supervising director from CAW observing their performance periodically and giving aid and support only upon request.

Still other, more ambitious ideas are being examined. One idea is to suggest to architects and construction companies that the community within which they are building should have a chance to influence and leave their imprint upon the structures. This means that an otherwise impersonal housing project might have a hallway or a driveway decorated with a design by its prospective tenants.

These suggestions are not readily accepted, and CAW has faced problems. There are those who think CAW's thrust is too aggressive and that disruptive rather than constructive ideas are emphasized. But there are others who think that most communities are strong enough to deal with controversial ideas and profit from shocks that shake complacency, encourage self-evaluation, and stimulate action for constructive change.

CAW offers a chance for communications that many communities want to take advantage of, and requests for help with new neighborhood projects are increasing.

TEACHERS AND WRITERS COLLABORATIVE
NEW YORK CITY

The Teachers and Writers Collaborative (TWC) was established in New York City in 1967 by a small group of poets and other writers who felt it would be feasible and useful for professional writers to work in schools to help young people develop their writing ability as one means of self-expression. A teacher, who was also one of the founding members of the group, initiated the program in his own classroom.

Since 1967, the Collaborative has expanded its operations to reach approximately one thousand children at all grade levels in some fifteen public schools. Four full-time and seventeen part-time professional writers are now working within these schools.

TWC focuses on the English curriculum in the public schools. The writers and the schools with which they work believe that changes in the language arts curriculum are needed to capture and sustain student interest and to develop creative capability. They have, therefore, developed an approach that is based on three major assumptions:

1. Children who are allowed to develop their use of language naturally, without the imposition of restrictive standards of usage and of grading and without arbitrary limits on content, tend to expand the boundaries of their verbal expression.

2. Attempting to teach technical skills of expression before a child has acquired an interest in and an attachment to language and literature tends to stifle his interest in expressing himself verbally. Grammatical and spelling skills can be developed much more readily after a child sees that they are related to his own concerns and his own enjoyment.

3. Children who write their own literature and who read the writings of other children are more likely to view all literature as an interesting and valuable way to deal creatively with one's experiences.

The Collaborative has placed its professionals in classrooms to work on a regular basis with teachers and students in exploring new ways of using language. Usually the professionals visit two different classes weekly. For example, they may spend the morning in a kindergarten and the afternoon with a fifth-grade class. The writers keep detailed diaries of their experiences. These diaries are the raw materials for the project's newsletters, curriculum materials, and books. They include the writer's commentaries and also samples of students' work.

TWC has increased its emphasis on encouraging very young children to express themselves creatively and to draw upon their own experiences and feelings for first dictating and later writing stories, poems, essays, and plays. Such experiences at an early age make many positive contributions to the growth of young children. They give a child confidence in his ability to use language; they help children to identify with "authors" as real people like themselves and to regard published writings as something that has a bearing on their own lives; and they build a foundation for using language as a means for personal satisfaction, for communication with others, and for clarification of one's own ideas and feelings.

The writers' commentaries and their collections of children's work have become testimonials to the Collaborative's efforts. The writers' diaries are painstakingly maintained, and some of them have been published as a record that may help teachers and others interested in encouraging young people to write. For example, *Wishes, Lies and Dreams*[3] includes some of the writings of a sixth-grade class from P.S. 41, along with the record kept by the poet who worked with this particular group of students. TWC is concerned, however, that reports such as these be regarded as stimuli rather than as formal patterns for teaching; it is disturbed by occasional

3. Kenneth Koch. *Wishes, Lies, and Dreams.* New York: Random House-Vintage, 1971, pap.

letters that indicate that teachers are trying to imitate almost precisely what the writer-teacher did when he worked with a particular group of young people.

This account of a Collaborative writer's experience with a sixth-grade class illustrates some of the individualism of TWC's techniques:

I drew a big wobbly, screwy shape on the blackboard. What is it? The United States. Good guess. Actually it is just one state. What state? It is not one of the fifty states. "It is a state of mind," one kid said. Wow! What a great idea. I said that actually I was thinking of it as the state of poetry like a new state added to the Union. The fifty-first state but that it exists in our imaginations only, so what they should do is draw a map and write a poem about the state of poetry. What is it like there? What do things look like? What does the sky look like? One student held up his hand and said, "I would rather write about the state of shock. It is just like the state of poetry for most people."

Some highly creative writing resulted from this approach:

In the State of Poetry, people eat poems. It feeds them information on how to be a poet. In the capital there is a sign with rhyme, "Welcome to the capital with your joys and tears and I hope you live happily every single year." The king of the state wears poetry from famous poets. They enjoy their life and that they do indeed. Whenever they get lazy, they have poetry to read. When they go to bed, all they do is dream. They dream of ice cream and jelly and poetry berries.

Away, away my wings took me and I fell into the land of poetry. First I crossed to the sun of Dreams, then I floated to the moon of sleep, then I rested till morning when my feet took me to the Poem Mountains. They were Beautiful. Then I crossed the sunny land of the pink People, then in the dark land of the Orange People I crossed everything anything one could wish for in my Beautiful Land of Poetry.

In another section of his diary, this same poet recounts his experience in enlisting the help of sixth-graders for his kindergarten poetry class. The ease with which they slipped into their roles as teacher aides suggested still another area of exploration.

A poet working at the Joan of Arc mini-school in East Harlem reported: "I often write a poem along with the class and share it with them. This helps to combat the idea that teachers make children do what they themselves cannot or will not do."

Another way to interest children in language is to encourage them to write their own reading books.

In the Manhattan midwinter of 1971 two elementary school teachers and I began an oral literature project. We wanted to cultivate and collect original literature with the children of two classes and out of that produce a new language arts curriculum. My colleagues were a fourth-grade teacher at P.S. 1 at the edge of Chinatown, and a fifth-grade teacher at P.S. 42, a few blocks east. In both schools there are many children who are not learning to read well or write competently and who feel no real sense of satisfaction in school. We thought if we made some class readers out of the children's own work, recorded the readers in a tape library, and designed a set of language exercises, we could inspire growth of the necessary skills. The key to our whole venture was special concentration on the natural competence of the children with spoken language and with vernacular stories and tales out of their own background and community. We wanted to free them, at least for a time, from the burden of writing and reading schoolbook English. By articulating a body of their literature, we planned to work back through reading, writing, and grammar.

The Collaborative has not found the going easy in the years it has been in existence. The director notes that a major problem has been working with schools that are highly structured and relatively inflexible. In such a situation it is difficult for the project's poets and writers to gain acceptance and be given an opportunity to work with children and with teachers.

Another difficulty has been the problem of recruiting writers who can work well with teachers and children. Professional writers are not necessarily good teachers. Some writers find it difficult to establish rapport with children and with teachers. If TWC's efforts are to be productive for both the teacher and the students, the writer must be accepted, by his adult colleagues and by children, as a valued member of the teaching staff. Although it is sometimes impossible to resolve differences in teaching styles, many Collaborative writers and poets have reported many experiences they feel were the result of productive, compatible relationships between themselves and the teacher, and between themselves and the students.

Two significant facts emerge from the material that has been accumulated by the Collaborative: (1) children can write joyfully, unexpectedly, creatively, and seriously when given the freedom to do so and (2) children can create work that other children and adults will enjoy. Traditional readers and grammar textbooks have often obscured these facts.

The role of the professional is to unearth and encourage talent, and this can be an especially rewarding role. It is beneficial—and unfortunately rare—for children to come into contact with such a creative adult. Children value talent and excellence just as adults do. Furthermore, professional writers manifest high enthusiasm and a profound respect for their craft, thereby increasing a child's desire to learn.

THE FILM CLUB
NEW YORK CITY

The creativity that the Teachers and Writers Collaborative found in the schools is certainly not limited to the written word. Children have proved again and again that they have a deep desire to express themselves, that their creativity is multi-faceted, and that unfamiliarity with a medium does not discourage them from experimenting with it and making exciting discoveries about it.

The Film Club grew out of a small pilot program started by three young adults who wanted to test the value of filmmaking as a learning tool for children. The success of their program led its founders to expand operations, and in 1967 the Club was incorporated as an independent program located in Manhattan's Lower East Side. Curious neighborhood kids frequently drop by the Club's store fronts to run their hands over the 16mm cameras and try to work the splicers in the cutting room.

Predictably, local interest has grown. With two store fronts on Rivington Street and with administrative and distribution offices in mid-Manhattan, the Film Club has given over fifteen hundred young people from the streets and the schools their first heady experience in filmmaking. The youngsters, working largely with their own creative imaginations, have made an average of three hundred films a year.

The operation of the Film Club is overseen by three adults who supervise the store fronts' many activities, arrange for the rental and distribution of more than one hundred selected teen-produced films, and explore possibilities for ways to expand activities. The project is financed by funds from the New York State Council of the Arts, foundations, and private grants. The expanded activities include:

☐ An ongoing videotape and filmmaking program with the children of Clinton Junior High School, an experimental school situated in midtown Manhattan with a student body drawn from the immediate area (popularly known as Hell's Kitchen) and from as far uptown as 125th Street.

☐ A film-viewing program for community libraries. This program utilizes a portable viewing unit called a moviebox, which is simple enough to be operated by young children interested in viewing films made by pre-teens and teenagers.

Two Super 8 filmmakers collaboratively plan their next scene.
ALFONSO BARRIOS

☐ Training programs for teachers in cooperation with New York University and New York's New School for Social Research.

☐ A cooperative teaching effort with schools. Experienced teenage filmmakers work with the school staff to help younger children learn the techniques of filmmaking.

☐ A Super 8 moviemaking project for children under twelve. Neighborhood pre-teens write their own scripts, shoot the films, and show them.

One reason for the Film Club's sustained popularity is the informality that characterizes its store fronts. It is easy to get involved, as can be seen from the following typical exchange of conversation:

Scene: (A boy strolls along outside the store front, stops, peers in, passes by. Then he turns and walks back toward the store front, looks again, hesitates a bit, and walks in. He sees some kids carrying camera equipment on their way to or from filming, and he sees others editing or putting on finishing touches. He walks to a young man who looks a little older than the others and who turns out to be the director of the store front.)

Boy: They say you let kids make films here.

Young man: Yeah, sure.

Boy: When can I start?

Young man: Soon as you know what you want to shoot and learn how to use the equipment and soon as you have your shooting script ready.

In the Film Club's store fronts, children are trusted implicitly with the expensive equipment as soon as they have been thoroughly instructed in its use and maintenance. No one reminds them constantly *not* to lose it, *not* to drop it, *not* to break it. "Trust earns trust," says the director of a store front for older children, "and we have had no major losses. The children are very careful with their material. Also they know that they won't be able to shoot with broken equipment."

The implications of taking on a project such as this and seeing it through are considerable when viewed in teenage terms. A young would-be producer, director, or writer is given one hundred feet of film and sent on his way. From the time he learns to work his camera, write a script, shoot the required footage and edit it, to the time he finally assembles it for viewing, he will have spent roughly six hundred hours on it—six hundred hours of frustration, elation, and determination on a project that will result in about ten minutes on the screen. The stress is great. He must be painfully selective in his choice of footage because his film is rationed. A word of encouragement here, a suggestion there, and he goes on. "We have thirty films going on at this moment," commented a store front director. "Nobody has lost interest yet."

The themes of the films and their treatment are as varied and unpredictable as the young creators themselves, and they range from bloody melodrama to pie-throwing comedy to journalistic commentary. *Bubby*, produced by an eighteen-year-old, is a study of the filmmaker's grandmother today, contrasted to her memories of herself as a young girl. Specialists consider it to be an effective and poignant statement of old age. *Day in the Life*, a six-minute piece by a fifteen-year-old, uses a well-loved Beatles lyric as a theme for sights and sounds of Manhattan's Lower East Side. A sixteen-year-old's *Teen Squad* reveals his ambivalence toward drug users.

In the Clinton School program mentioned earlier, ten pre-teens have been taking an elective videotape course with the Film Club. The course provides a carefully ordered, practical, and thorough orientation in videotaping. The students become completely familiar with camera, videotaping recording deck, and tape editing. They view tapes created by other young people; they discuss what they like and don't like about these tapes, and what they would have done differently. After this they write their own scripts.

When a script is written and discussed, the young director chooses the ingredients that his particular script calls for—actors, props, crew members, locations—and is ready to start. By the time the tape is edited, some fifty to one hundred hours of work have been devoted to the project.

The Film Club is also helping to teach English in a new way. Children beginning to learn English as a second language in an elementary school in Chinatown use Super 8 equipment to make two-minute films about anything that interests them. They write their own scripts, and because they must "sound right," the young children work painstakingly to make their sentences correct. The result is an almost unconscious absorption of English usage and an exciting introduction to an intriguing new medium.

Of special interest for educators is the Club's work with schools, using experienced teen filmmakers to work with the school staff in teaching filmmaking.

FOLKLORE MAGAZINES

The idea of producing a magazine has a fascination for numbers of young people, and over the years youth and their teachers have turned out a great variety of class and school publications. These publications vary widely in format, in purpose, in extent of student involvement, in freedom of expression and choice of content, in quality of content, in relevance to student interests and needs, and in awareness of how youth-produced publications may serve community interests.

Some recent efforts to explore the broad range of possibilities offered by youth involvement in magazine publication have resulted in the development of three significant and quite unique publications—*Foxfire*, *Hoyekiya*, and *The Fourth Street i*.

FOXFIRE
RABUN GAP, GEORGIA

Foxfire was born in an English class taught by a man who was convinced that English should and could be a moving, living language for the young people in the small Appalachian town of Rabun Gap, Georgia. Pursuing his conviction, he suggested that his students think about putting out a magazine. Questions had to be considered: What would they write about? What was unique about their lives and their community that they could share with people outside the school? Where and how would they collect the information and ideas to write about?

The publication that developed was a quaint and delightfully personal folklore magazine that has not only brought satisfaction to its publishers and local readers but has also put the small Georgia town on the map. *Foxfire* is a quarterly magazine with a circulation of five thousand. To provide content for their magazine issues, students of Rabun Gap High School go into their mountain community with notebooks, cameras, and tape recorders to capture and preserve, in words and in pictures, a way of life that would otherwise disappear and leave no record.

The Appalachian backwoodsman and the mountain farmer come alive in *Foxfire*. Vivid characters emerge from its glossy, well laid-out pages—people like Aunt Arie, a spry eighty-five-year-old who lives alone, fetches her own water, and does her own cooking; an old farmer who shows the young people how to make an ox-yoke puzzle; a traveling evangelist of some years ago whose way of life is recalled through a collection of his own materials loaned to the students by his daughter. Copies of *Foxfire* are filled with unexpected treasures: "Log Cabin Building," "Planting by the Signs," "Churning Your Own Butter," and "Recipes from the Mountains."

When *Foxfire* began in the spring of 1967, it was not an integral part of the curriculum at Rabun Gap. Work on the magazine was done during lunch hours, on holidays, and after school. But after its early and remarkable success, it became the focus of an elective journalism class taught by the teacher who initiated the project. Through instruction and on-the-job experience, young people from the eighth through the twelfth grades learn the skills essential for a successful and continuing publication. They learn to write and to edit, they learn how to conduct an interview, and they learn production and business management aspects of publication. At every stage, their performance is evaluated by senior student editors and/or by the teacher. Students move to positions of increased responsibility as their performance improves; sustained good work earns them a coveted place on the Senior Editorial Board.

Foxfire has helped to build strong relationships between the high school and the community. The young people painstakingly record on film, on tape, and in notebooks the knowledge of the adults in Rabun Gap. In many other communities throughout the country there is equally rich and interesting information to be preserved. Often, however, knowledge is left unexplored in the memories of older citizens. The visible evidences important for reconstructing a picture of life in an earlier day—the quilts, the churns, the kerosene lamps, the horsehair sofas—have been stashed away or simply ignored, their significance unrecognized. But that is not true in Rabun Gap. The young people give their elders opportunities to talk about their memories and to display the still remaining physical evidences of their earlier lives or the lives of their own parents and grandparents. In the process, the young people not only gather material for their magazine but also enrich their own experiences. For the older people and for those much younger, *Foxfire* has provided some rare, invaluable, and mutually satisfying cross-age contacts.

There have been several interesting developments related to the success of the magazine. The *Foxfire Book,* vintage selections from the first five years of the magazine, was published by Anchor/Doubleday in 1972; it was so popular that *Foxfire 2* was issued in 1973 (also published by Anchor/Doubleday). The royalties are going toward the creation of a museum-archive-craft center. Many of the *Foxfire* tapes—recorded student interviews with members of the Appalachian community—have been purchased by the Smithsonian Institution.

HOYEKIYA
PINE RIDGE, SOUTH DAKOTA

The *Foxfire* experiment soon began to stimulate replication. In South Dakota, on the Pine Ridge Indian Reservation, a community worker with a background in publishing had been toying with the idea of compiling the legends and literature of the Dakota people. Ideas Inc., a private agency committed to initiating development projects in depressed areas of the United States and abroad, approached the developer of *Foxfire* to see if he thought a folk-culture magazine would be feasible for the Sioux children of Pine Ridge. The result was a magazine titled *Hoyekiya,* which in the Dakota language means a voice that cries out or speaks from the heart.

The *Foxfire* imprint on *Hoyekiya* is unmistakable. In it there is revealed the same desire to record the time-honored customs of an older generation. This may be due in part—but only in part—to the fact that early in the development of *Hoyekiya,* two of the high school staff members from Pine Ridge visited Rabun Gap to exchange ideas with the student editors of *Foxfire.*

The first issue of *Hoyekiya* celebrated sun dance, an event that takes place in August and is the most solemn of ceremonies for the ten thousand Sioux in the area. The young staff recorded the significance of the sacred sun dance songs as explained by Edgar Red Cloud of the Oglala Sioux Tribe, chief singer at the sun dance:

Now I wanna sing that song just before the sun dance starts. When they get up. They all sleep in the hut. When they wake up, this song is sung by the leader of the group to dance to in the sun dance. For this, I don't use no drum. It's not supposed to be sung with drum. This is a more sacred song. Everytime I sing that, it makes me feel bad that I sing it.

On other pages there are recipes for Wojapi or poipaya, Ciya Ka or peppermint tea, and more tales from Sioux elders.

My mother said she was twelve years old the time Crazy Horse was killed and she said the Indians were moving from Fort Robinson when they killed him.

Another issue dealt with autumn and the Sioux way to prepare for winter. The Lakota and other sub-tribes of the Sioux have unique and time-tested methods for beating the cold.

The editorial staff of *Hoyekiya* is drawn from the high schools in the district, including the county and parochial schools as well as schools operated by the Bureau of Indian Affairs. At any given time, there will be between five and fifteen staff members. From the start, staff members have been involved in every stage of the production of the magazine. "Of course they needed guidance at the very beginning," said *Hoyekiya*'s technical advisor, "but now all I do is handle Internal Revenue Service and copyright matters. The young staffers tend to work at their own pace, and meeting deadlines is not stressed. They react adversely to undue pressures, and I have been mindful of that at all times."

Hoyekiya provides an inspiring example to young American Indians whose quest for identity is as anguished as that of other minorities.

THE FOURTH STREET I
NEW YORK CITY

Like *Foxfire* and *Hoyekiya*, *The Fourth Street i* was designed to serve a particular community. In this case, the community is an area in Manhattan's Lower East Side, and the magazine takes its name from the blocks where the publication originated. The magazine's publishers are teenagers from the area, most of whom are Puerto Rican.

Today the community feels that *The Fourth Street i* is really their magazine, that it belongs to the community. But it took some time for the feeling to develop; the initial reaction to the project was one of apathy.

The first issue came out in the winter of 1970, a year after the idea had been proposed. By that time people were interested enough to take the magazine home, to show it to their neighbors, and to express some pride in it. But they did not feel close enough to it to criticize or to point out what the staff itself identified as shortcomings in the first issue: it lacked the flavor of the streets, the flavor of life as the people knew it; it spoke *about* the people but not really *to* them. This could have been caused, in part, by the fact that not many of the area's teenagers had become fully involved in the development of the first issue of the *i*. For a number of reasons, much of the responsibility for producing this first magazine fell to adult supervisors, with adult professional help on production aspects.

But with the publication of the second issue, subtitled "Operation Rainbow," the situation began to change. An enthusiastic Puerto Rican teenager took over as editor early in 1970, and in a spontaneous taped message to the staff, he expressed some of his feelings about what could be done:

I'm a New Yorker, man, and I feel that she's hung up. . . . It's a hung up world—hung up on welfare and junk. Come on, baby, get off that bag. You know where it's at. Man, just join me, my crew, we can show the world where we are at—by art, poetry, and other ways. . . . We have a small staff of four people including myself, and I'd like to recruit some more Puerto Rican kids and old people to help us in our cause. . . . We have a big cause. We want to show people our culture, our background. . . .

The staff began using the community as their source of material, and when this happened, *The Fourth Street i* began to be what it had set out to be—a publication deeply rooted in the community it seeks to represent.

The third issue, subtitled "The Stoop," marked the first time the magazine had been written, illustrated, edited, and laid out by the young editorial staff without outside resources. "We even used our own typewriter, and it's crummy, but we like it better this way."

In an editorial in "The Stoop," a young girl, who also typed most of the copy for the magazine, wrote about what working on *The Fourth Street i* meant to her:

It's hard for me to explain the way I feel about the magazine, because I don't feel the magazine is just a bunch of paper put together. It means more to me than that. I worked on the second one and I worked on this one, for a year now almost. And each time it's a different experience, a different feeling I have from it, like a second birth you can say. It's a baby in which I have the power to mold, create, and bring to life all the characteristics of the Lower East Side—the richness of the sun outside and the pain of a starving child. So to my baby, I said: "Thank you for letting me be so proud and full of joy every time you exist."

Issues of *The Fourth Street i* include poems, stories, articles, photographs, drawings, and comic strips. Some of the material is written in Spanish; some in English. When it seems appropriate, the same article or story may appear in both languages. Contributions come from adults—including some who are on welfare—from young children, and from teen-

A page from a bilingual cartoon story in the *Fourth Street i,* illustrated by Ramon Rojas.

agers. No effort is made to refine the language of the streets and the tenements. One boy, writing about "My Street," said:

In my street there were cats and mouse. There in the hallway there were junkies. I said mother do we have to live in here I said. The super did not give a hell of a damn what has happen to us because he had kids like they were bad. There were furniture on the roof floor. They set it on fire and all of a sudden the fire start to smell. We were asleep. My father woke up. I and my sister had to call the firemen. Then he told us to head for the stairs so we did. The next day it was beautiful.

Contributors tell their stories simply and truthfully, without artfulness.

I am from Bayamon, P.R.
I was abandoned at the age of 11 years.
I was born in 1936.
I am 34 years old actually,
I brought myself up.
Today I have made myself a man
and I am father of a son
who is my pride.
On June 4, I was attacked
unjustly by the T.P.F in
1968 on 9 Street.
Four years ago, I formed a group
called the Lucky Swings.
I cooperate with the community
of 9 Street.
I have my wife who is very good.
Her name is Maria Maysonet.
This is my story.

One little boy wrote about what it is like to be white in a black neighborhood:

The Black people talk about the way white people call them names. But I do not complain when the Black people call us names like white pig and Whitey.

At one time, the eighteen-year-old editor-in-chief wrote about education and what it means to him:

"I am pro education but I am anti school. . . . If I could share my experience with one other person, teach him what I'd learned, it'd be outasight."

In another article, a street-wise fifth-grader offered his opinion about drugs and illustrated it with a drawing of an array of drugs and a nurse bending over a corpse:

New York is a city with drug addicts. I do not like to live in a place like this. I would rather be dead than live in a place like this! There are a lot of people dead because of drugs and I don't like it!

Kick the habit before it kicks you dead!

The young staff, which currently numbers six, is firmly united in their thinking about the purpose of the magazine. "In the beginning not too many people read our magazine," said one staff member, "but now they do. Now when they read something they've written or their friends have written, they feel good about it."

Staff members are constantly moving about within their community, encouraging people to put down on paper or speak into a tape recorder what they feel and think. Sometimes they suggest ideas, but nearly all the contributed material is the product of original thinking. Above all, the staff wants the magazine to be a mirror for the thoughts of people—a means for helping them realize that their way of thinking and feeling and living is unique and beautiful:

We have people with something in the way they look, the way they talk and the way they dress. With all of these things together, you get a sound, a certain expression, a beauty, something you don't get on Park Avenue. It's so real you can touch it, you can feel it, it's in the air. It's the big voice of the poor trying to climb higher till they're on top.

(Excerpt from an editorial in "Operation Rainbow")

The effect the magazine has had in helping the community to build a positive self-image is evident in such comments as:

I didn't know there was so much talent in the neighborhood.

I've known him all my life but I didn't know he had all that in him.

The Fourth Street i now reaches schools in many parts of the country, and it is being used by a growing number of schools in the local school district. The content of the magazine provides information and insight to its readers. One issue of *The i* dealt with Puerto Rico and was based, in part, on a visit to Puerto Rico by the staff. The staff also added material describing Puerto Rican culture, heritage, and life in the New York Puerto Rican ghetto. The end result was a publication that provided Puerto Ricans—in other parts of the country as well as in New York—with literature emerging from experience. The members of the staff hope that their magazine will provide minority groups in schools throughout the country with reading that is directly related to their lives. But they have another purpose, too, and that is to reach people throughout the country who are *not* of a minority group, reach them with the hope of building understanding, respect, and some feeling of empathy.

An impressive measure of the value accorded to *The Fourth Street i* is the fact that the local school board for the district in which the magazine is published is buying ten thousand copies of the Puerto Rican issue to distribute to every junior high school in the district. The magazine will be used, for example, in bilingual studies, in English, and in social studies classes. This represents an investment of several thousand dollars in the work of young people, many of whom have been or are "turned off" from schools.

The young editors of *The i* have succeeded in creating a significant threefold relationship with their community: (*1*) they have provided a vehicle of expression, (*2*) they have brought the schools and the community closer together by providing a two-way exchange of information and ideas, and (*3*) they have helped the community to develop a more positive self-image. Furthermore, the young workers have become knowledgeable in every aspect of magazine planning and production and take complete responsibility for getting out each issue. They are currently engaged in a special training project —going out into the local public schools to interest other young people in the project and to help them learn the skills that they themselves have already acquired.

A FURTHER WORD

As suggested at the beginning of this chapter, the need to communicate is a vital and a continuing human need. It is a part of growing up; it is a part of being mature. The various ways youth are communicating successfully emphasize some important facts:

☐ There are innumerable ways to communicate, and young people are capable of using them creatively and effectively.

☐ Collaboration with skilled professionals can help to develop interest in creative self-expression and can provide expert assistance in developing needed skills.

☐ Many forms of self-expression can be used to bring people closer together in cooperative efforts to cope with common problems and to experience satisfaction in creative activity.

☐ In the area of communication, as in many other areas, young people are constantly demonstrating their ability to function as competent, compassionate, and responsible individuals.

YOUTH
as resources for youth

Everyone here wants to change in one way or another.
But we are all uncertain of just who we want to be.
So we experiment, we open up to ourselves and
really listen.

We are here because there is no refuge, finally, from
ourselves. Until a person confronts himself, in the eyes
and hearts of others, he is running. Until he suffers
them to share his secrets, he has no safety from them.

The Aides have helped to develop a good social climate.
They've been able to take boys aside and counsel
them and take disruptive influences out of the group.

Young people have always used each other to test and exchange information, understanding, skills, ideas, friendship, and love. But only recently have they begun to work together intensively to help each other cope with the critical problems that trouble them. With dedication and competence that often surprise their elders, they are working to help one another deal with and overcome problems that adults have usually been expected to solve—problems such as delinquency, vagabondage, physical or mental disability, retardation, and slow learning, problems such as the need to be a respected and influential part of the total society and the need to have political representation within that society.

There are a number of reasons why these organized youth-helping-youth efforts are developing. For one, many young people feel—and often actually are—cut off from the adult community. This is partly a matter of communication. The problem of communication between young people and adults is not a new one, but it is new to each generation and the rapidity of change in today's society accentuates the gap between the young and the not so young. Young people are doubtful that adults can understand their problems; they are wary about exposing themselves to their elders and skeptical about receiving any real understanding and help.

On the other hand, the same factors that have served to cut youth off from the adult community—for example, the acceleration of the pace of change, the weakening of family bonds, the increase of such impersonal communications media as television and film—have also made young people more aware of themselves as a distinct group, as a unit possessing important and valuable characteristics that supplement and complement those of the adult community. Young people are developing a sense of shared problems; they recognize that the problems of some youths are in many cases the problems of all. And they are discovering that simply being young oneself has a certain unique value for helping to solve the problems of other youths.

Society is discovering the same thing. Evidence collected from projects where young people serve as resources for people their own age or younger strongly suggests that just being young is valuable in dealing with the problems of the young.

In this chapter are descriptions of several projects in which young people have undertaken to help one another. In these projects, as in other youth involvement projects described in this volume, effective adult support comes from those who have confidence in youth's ability to exercise initiative, to be creative, and to operate responsibly. School personnel are frequently among those supportive adults. But in the projects described in this particular chapter, there is a slightly different focus that makes it extremely important for supportive adults to assess very carefully the roles they can play without distorting the basic concept involved—*youth as resources for youth.*

HELPING RUNAWAYS AND OTHER TROUBLED YOUTH

YOUTH ADVOCATES
SEATTLE, WASHINGTON

Youth Advocates is a small, relatively unstructured program designed to help troubled teenagers from Seattle's predominantly white middle-class and lower-middle-class neighborhoods. It grew out of a summer Open Door Clinic in which an adult volunteer staff of two hundred and twenty served eleven hundred clients a month. Three high school students approached the Open Door Clinic with the suggestion that they could work within the community to find youths with problems and send them to the Clinic for help. Their suggestion was not accepted because they were minors and couldn't legally work for the Clinic and also because they lived fifteen miles away. But a young social worker who was to become Project Director of Youth Advocates and who was then active in the Clinic felt that this youth initiative should be encouraged. He was impressed by the ability of young people to help their contemporaries and disturbed by the general assumption that only college graduates and/or professionals were qualified to assist troubled youngsters. He told the young people that if they were willing to work in their own community, some fifteen miles from the Clinic, he would work with them and give them whatever help he could. The young people were receptive to his suggestion, and a youth outreach project was established in West Seattle.

Youth Advocates was formed early in 1969 with a twenty-man Board of Directors, nine of whom were under twenty-one. The functions of the Board are the same now as when it was first established: to raise funds, to act as consultants, and to help maintain a referral system that draws from business, educational, legal, medical, and social work resources. The day-to-day power lies in the hands of the young staff; as a group, they are responsible for both the direction and the operation of their program. The final responsibility, however, rests with the Project Director.

From the beginning the program has had certain basic functions. It focuses primarily on street-oriented young people, and it provides them with houses where they can depend on finding a door always open to them, recreational facilities and peer contacts, a staff skilled in human relations, although not necessarily and not usually on a professional level, and encouragement for voluntary participation and for self-help. The drop-in is always encouraged to define his own problem, but he is not necessarily asked to discover a solution for it. The available services are explained by the peer group—a procedure that tends to win the confidence of young drop-ins who have become skeptical about adult attitudes toward their problems and about adult efforts to be helpful.

The project began with one rented house. Furniture was

purchased inexpensively from a Catholic charitable organization. The project soon expanded to include four houses located in different parts of West Seattle. In the course of its history, the project has maintained houses in six different locations in that area. Youth Advocates now has only three physical facilities, but the services it offers are greater in breadth and depth than ever before. Two of the facilities are drop-in centers operated in the tradition of Youth Advocates' first house. The third facility contains the program's administrative headquarters, the offices of a new intensive help program called Senior Advocates, and a short-term foster home. These three components—the drop-in centers, the Senior Advocates program, and the foster home—are the core of Youth Advocates today.

THE DROP-IN CENTERS   Becky is a staff member at Crossroads, one of the drop-in centers. She wears a maxi coat and round moon glasses; she loves cats and believes in reincarnation; she has an apartment of her own.

Through Crossroads, Becky is involved in the problems of her contemporaries as a helper and a counselor. She also trains other young people in ways to give assistance to youths with such problems as drug-taking, alienation, running away from home, anti-social behavior, aggression, and loneliness. Becky, along with other young people, deals with the addict, the runaway, and the boy or girl who just wants a friendly place to go to in the evening. They have been through many problems themselves (for example, seven staffers are runaways—or have been), and they feel that their own experiences make them uniquely qualified to help others. They know that the center's success depends largely on them, and they accept the fact that the job demands dedication and hard work.

Each drop-in center is overseen by a young coordinator. The houses where centers are located are not residential, although the coordinator usually lives there. Houses are open from 6 p.m. to 10 p.m. on weekdays and from 7 p.m. to 2 a.m. on Fridays and Saturdays. A number of staff members are always on duty to accommodate those who drop in, and teamwork among staff members is considered very important.

The young clients include the disengaged, the underactive, and the isolated—young people who are no longer able to relate to a former peer group but have been unable to find another. Some of them are involved in drug dealing or handling stolen goods; many are runaways. The number of clients in a house on any one night averages about fifty. On Friday nights the staff is reinforced to cope with end-of-the-week exuberance that sometimes accentuates such problems as the use of drugs and alcohol.

No member of the staff is ever permitted to come into one of the houses if he or she is high on drugs or alcohol; clients are similarly restricted. Drug dealing and the handling of stolen items are strongly discouraged. If any of the clients begin to behave in a violent or anti-social manner, the house is closed temporarily. The inevitable personality problems among staff members are managed kindly but firmly. Efforts are made to resolve problems, but if these efforts fail, a staff member may be asked to look for work elsewhere. The general atmosphere is one of responsibility and common sense, and this leads to a feeling of relaxed stability. This is partly a result of the supportive, friendly, but firm attitudes about responsible behavior.

Staff members are generally chosen from two sources: clients who indicate a willingness and an ability to undertake the necessary responsibilities and young people outside the centers who learn about staff openings through newspaper articles or by word of mouth. Members of the staff are selected carefully and then trained for their jobs. Before being selected, the prospective staffer must be interviewed and approved by a group of current staff members. After selection, a new staff member undergoes a thorough training that includes several months of in-service training combined with a pre-service program provided by the Youth Advocates Training Guild.

The Training Guild, developed by the Youth Advocates Board of Directors for the purpose of staff development, utilizes the skills and talents of young staff representatives and of resource persons from the community. The Guild is composed of two Board members, one staff representative from each drop-in center, and three community people. Participants from the Board and the community are expected to bring their expertise to the training program's planning phase, and the youth staff representatives are expected to provide data regarding the emergency training needs of their individual programs. Thus, the training is constantly being adapted to the current problems of the centers.

Each center has a training committee or a training coordinator, and a member of each center's committee, or its coordinator, participates in the Training Guild. Each house staff is responsible for training new staff members and is free to select the training program best suited to its needs. The chairman of the Training Guild is responsible for coordinating the programs.

There are three main phases in each training program: (1) "How-to-do-it," which teaches crisis intervention techniques, use of the telephone for coping with problems, and counseling on such problems as drugs, family difficulties, and running away from home; (2) "What we are doing to each other?" which includes training in interstaff dynamics, the importance of trust, and how to distinguish and choose between staff needs and personal needs; (3) "How do we deal with each other?" which involves learning about making referrals, interagency dynamics, interhouse dynamics, organizational issues, and community relations.

The twenty-hour training program for new staff is spread over a period of about three weeks and reflects the imagination and talent shown by planners and trainers in developing effective teaching-learning methods and techniques. Role playing, for example, tele-training, lectures, and tours are some of the approaches used in sessions that may last from two hours to two days.

The training program serves three main purposes:

1. It exposes the prospective staff member to the different ways staff groups work, and it shows him how the centers actually function. It also helps him determine whether he really wants to be on the staff and, if so, where he would best fit in.

2. It helps the trainee develop background for handling the kinds of cases that the center usually encounters.

3. It enables the staff to evaluate the applicant's potential ability, or lack of it.

Training begins with a two-hour orientation session. This covers the history of the center and Youth Advocates, tells the applicant something of the house and its basic programs, and gives him an idea of how the center operates. Time is provided for the trainee and the coordinator to discuss the trainee's feelings about the center.

The next stage is a two-hour drop-in training and evaluation session. This starts with some basic training in handling crowds (indoors and out) and in handling conflicts within the drop-in area and is followed by a discussion of the purposes and functions of the drop-in staff. The trainee learns about the kinds of experiences he may encounter with drop-ins and how the staff should react to crises. A large part of this session consists of role playing various incidents such as the arrival of an acid bummer, an abuse-of-the-house situation, and an example of drugs-on-the-property.

Each trainee is then assigned to a trainer and goes with him to a center at one of its busiest times. The trainee is there mainly to observe, although he may be given a job such as keeping a head count sheet. When the shift is over, trainer and trainee talk over the evening's occurrences and discuss in depth the subtleties of actions and reactions. The trainee next attends a two-hour counseling, training, and evaluation session, which acquaints him with any interstaff systems the counseling staff may have set up to handle various types of crises. The trainee then attends a general staff meeting.

Finally, the current staff holds an evaluation session. By this time most of the unsuitable trainees will have abandoned the program, and in this session the staff discusses each of the remaining trainees and decides whether to recommend the trainee for staff membership or to advise him to find an outlet in some other group or organization. If the decision is made to recommend the trainee, then the entire staff group votes on his acceptance and decides where he will actually work. After the staff meeting, the trainee is asked to meet with the group to discuss their findings and to raise his own questions.

The sense of purpose and stability that pervades each of the houses is a major contribution of the Training Guild that cannot be overstressed. Although the staff for any one house usually includes no one over twenty years old, the Training Guild accepts each member on an equal footing and maintains a sense of common purpose with the adults who come in to work as colleagues and consultants. It is one of the strengths of the program that it is able to bring in adults to work with young people who have been alienated from older people and from the institutions of the adult world but who, through this working relationship, discover that many people older than themselves also have a contribution to make to the solution of youth problems. Interestingly enough, parents of a number of the young people are involved in the program.

It is also interesting to note that the training has taken on a new dimension because the young people who participated in setting it up have themselves become trainers, working outside of Youth Advocates as well as within it. The high reputation that the training programs have earned has led many local groups to ask training teams to help them deal with other youth problems. Youth Advocates, therefore, sparked the realization that a new field of work is opening up for the young—helping the adult community to become aware of the various facets of youth problems and to be open to new ways for solving them.

THE SENIOR ADVOCATES   The Senior Advocates are the staff members, now twenty in number, who handle individual cases that require more in-depth consultation and care than is ordinarily provided at the drop-in centers. These Advocates are usually older and more experienced than the other staffers working in the centers. They deal mainly with runaways and with those who have recently been through juvenile court proceedings. The Seniors attempt to draw from each of these youngsters a reasonable understanding of what his realistic options are. Then, if he chooses among the options available, they try to suggest the most promising ways to pursuing the direction he has selected. Next, the Senior Advocates serve as "resource hustlers" by helping the young person find the kinds of professional help needed—legal, medical, or psychiatric. As "resource hustlers," they also help him meet other needs such as clothing, food, and a job. One of the chief aims of the Advocates is to keep youngsters out of the local detention center for juveniles. It is customary for an Advocate to work with a case until the youth is legally placed in a setting where he seems likely to work out his problems successfully.

SHORT-TERM FOSTER HOME   One of the serious problems that Youth Advocates faced during the early days of its operations was its inability to physically accommodate many young runaways who were desperately in need of help. Staff members often let these troubled youngsters stay in their own homes for a few days, but the organization had no legal right to keep a young person in its custody. Without immediate attention, runaways would often drift off before Youth Advocates had time to do anything substantial to help them.

To remedy this situation, Youth Advocates set up a licensed foster home in the large house that also serves as its administration building. Youth Advocates feels very strongly, however, that its purpose is not to serve as a long-term foster parent, and that no young person should become overly dependent on the food and shelter that Youth Advocates can provide. It has, therefore, adopted a rule that no individual may spend more than thirty days in its foster home. The organization is considering a further rule that would limit residence to those young people for whom there are no other options. These restrictions would rarely work a hardship on any needy young person because, in most cases, the Advocates can place a young person in a suitable, accredited residence within two weeks. Meanwhile, its foster home has enabled Youth Advocates to make services immediately available to many of the most severe cases of alienated youth.

Youth Advocates has been a successful venture, and there are several important elements in that success:

☐ The character and influence of the Director. The Director, a young man of commitment and imagination, has great sympathy for, understanding of, and confidence in young people. The agency is so structured that the Director and the youthful staff have ultimate control over policy; the Board's function is consultative and advisory.

☐ Genuine youth participation. Young people really operate the houses; they are the ones who make on-the-spot decisions and deal with the problems. Through their participation in the Training Guild and on the Board, young people also play a major role in the development of policy. The agency's effectiveness depends in large part on its ability to respond to problems with the immediacy, fluidity, and flexibility of youth.

☐ The effectiveness of the training program provided through the Training Guild. This program uses the knowledge and talent of current staff members for helping to design and participate in training programs for potential staff members.

It contributes to the development of self-discipline, personal responsibility, and a sense of stability within the various houses. And it provides a channel of intercommunication between young people and the adults who come in to serve as consultants and colleagues.

☐ An association with adults that is built on a basis of common concerns. This is fostered through the Training Guild and the consultant-referral system and has helped to free many young people from their negative attitudes about the adult world and their feelings of alienation from it.

☐ Opportunities for changes in relationships and roles. The relationship between the youth staff and young drop-ins is not a static one; the staff helps drop-ins who may, at a later time, themselves become helpers for troubled youth.

☐ The breadth of staff responsibilities and the opportunity for personal growth. Young people are involved in both demanding and satisfying ways at all levels of the organization, and the opportunity for taking on still greater responsibility is always open.

☐ A new look at the meaning of self-discipline. Both the training program and the requirements of the work itself emphasize the need for self-discipline. This emphasis has led many young people to a reassessment of self-discipline as it relates to behavior in the larger community and to an awareness of the idea that there is a reconcilable relationship between self-discipline and personal freedom.

The single greatest problem that Youth Advocates has faced during its existence has been a chronic and serious shortage of money. The organization has had some fortunate breaks, as, for example, when admirers of the program made it possible for the Advocates to pay a dollar a year rent for the large house that serves as headquarters. Usually, however, there is barely enough money to pay for rent and utilities at the other facilities, and not enough to pay any salaries at all. There are six VISTA volunteers on the Youth Advocates staff, but nearly all of the one hundred-odd staffers, including the Director, are volunteers. One of the most unfortunate results of the money shortage is that many of the staffers are forced to take on second and third part-time jobs to support themselves. The result is exhaustion, which cannot help but affect the efficiency of even the most dedicated staff worker.

The annual budget for Youth Advocates comes chiefly from occasional grants and contributions, and most of it is spent on upkeep. The group is seeking federal funds to cover the amount considered necessary for the operation of a continuing and maximally effective program, but it is uncertain how much, if any, of this money will be provided.

Other Programs

Youth Advocates in Seattle is just one of a number of programs for troubled young people. There are "crisis centers"[1] of various kinds in many other cities where the problems of young people are severe, for example in Ann Arbor, Michigan; Atlanta, Georgia; Boston, Massachusetts; Chicago, Illinois; Cleveland, Ohio; Palo Alto, California; Phoenix, Arizona; and Washington, D.C. A few of these projects are described briefly here.

☐ Number Nine in New Haven, Connecticut, is a particularly interesting project in which all the staff are under twenty-five years old and live in an old sixteen-room house. Like many of these programs, Number Nine grew out of a twenty-four-hour emergency telephone service. In addition to operating the telephone service, Number Nine now has a store front for recreation and counseling and a house for short-term

---

1. Those who would like further information about other youth-helping-youth groups may wish to secure a copy of *A Directory of Hotlines, Switchboards, and Related Services*. It is available for $2. from THE EXCHANGE, 311 Cedar Avenue South, Minneapolis, Minnesota 55404, is organized by state, and includes addresses and telephone numbers.

room and board. Staff members also go out into the New Haven community to give on-the-spot help with problems such as drug addiction.

☐   HELP in Philadelphia, Pennsylvania, has focused on the fact that young people on the streets are often the victims of a wide variety of misinformation. It was founded early in 1970 by a group of young people who, having been arrested themselves, knew how difficult it is to find a trusted person from whom they could seek aid and advice. HELP has dedicated itself to becoming expert on many of the problems that young people seem likely to encounter. Although, like Youth Advocates and Number Nine, it maintains some clinical services and can find runaways a place to sleep, the very heart of HELP is its twenty-four-hour telephone service that handles upwards of three hundred calls a day about problems such as drug addiction, pregnancy, and possible suicide. The telephone service offers a comforting voice and objective information, and it provides access to necessary resources—volunteer doctors, lawyers, and psychiatrists.

☐   Youth to Youth on Drug Abuse Education in San Francisco, California works directly through the San Francisco schools. Older high school students have organized themselves to use peer pressure to discourage younger high school students from becoming involved with drugs. They have conducted teach-ins, prepared multi-media instructional aids, and organized in-depth studies of the drug scene.

☐   Drugs, runaways, and delinquency are probably the most obvious problems faced by today's youth, but they are by no means the only problems that have elicited organized responses from young people. Consider, for example, the problems of the emotionally disturbed and the physically handicapped. The Friend to Friend program sponsored by the Jewish Social Service Agency in Rockville, Maryland, arranges for high school boys and girls to spend several hours each week for a whole year with handicapped persons their own age, on a one-to-one basis. Some magical things have happened. A seventeen-year-old boy in a wheelchair was taken to a museum for the first time in his life. (This was also his first outing without his parents.) A twenty-year-old girl with cerebral palsy learned how to bake. Two retarded girls enjoyed a slumber party with their volunteers. For the handicapped, these are significant achievements that give them satisfaction today and hope for the future.

COUNSELING

PEER COUNSELING PROGRAM
PALO ALTO, CALIFORNIA

A Peer Counseling Program for secondary schools is operated under the sponsorship of the Stanford University Department of Psychiatry and the Palo Alto Unified School District. Begun as a pilot program in 1970 and scheduled to continue through June 1975, this is a community mental health project for youth.

THE DROP-IN CENTERS   The program trains high school and junior high school students (grades seven through twelve, ages twelve through eighteen) to provide a wide variety of services to their fellow students. Services include helping solve personal problems; teaching social skills; developing friendships; tutoring in academic areas; giving information about jobs, volunteer opportunities, and mental health resources in the communities; and helping alienated youth make positive contact with the adult world.

The basic structure of the training program is a small group organization. Over a period of ten weeks, eight to ten trainees meet for two to five days per week for two hours, working under the supervision of mental health professionals. This part of the training program includes many opportunities for students to take part in role-playing activities and to function as group leaders, observers, and participants. Next the trainees take on their first work assignment—meeting with sixth-grade students near the end of the school year, a time when these students are sensitive to their fall transfer to junior high school. Peer counselors meet with small groups of sixth-graders to encourage them to discuss their feelings about the transition to junior high school and to inform them that peer counselors will be available to help them in the fall. No adult supervisor is present. Later, in their training groups, counselors discuss their experiences, the problems they encountered, and ways in which they might deal with them.

The effort to recruit peer counselors for training is not intensive, but information is made available to seven thousand students in the three junior high schools and the three senior high schools in the Palo Alto Unified School District. One hundred and sixty-two students entered the initial program; one hundred and fifty-five completed it. Informal evaluations by adults and by students indicate that the program has been beneficial for both the peer counselors and the students with whom they work. More extensive evaluation procedures are now underway.

Indicative of the interest in the program are the increasing requests for the services of the counselors. Also significant are the possibilities that are opening up for an even more varied type of program. For example, parents of students in mentally retarded classes requested a meeting regarding possible help. Elementary school teachers have asked for specific services. School district personnel want to explore the possibilities of peer counselors helping students who have attendance problems.

The Peer Counseling Program is the first stage of a hoped-for comprehensive school mental health plan. The long-range objective is a self-sustaining Peer Counseling Program that can function within the school system with minimum involvement of outside mental health professionals. This would include establishing a training program for teachers and counselors that would provide the help they themselves would need to train and supervise students as peer counselors.

THE UNWINDING ROOM
PHILADELPHIA, PENNSYLVANIA

The Unwinding Room is located at Saint Maria Goretti High School, a Catholic girls' school in Philadelphia. When it started in 1971, it was sponsored by the Diagnostic and Rehabilitation Center of Philadelphia; it is now sponsored by the Archdiocese of Philadelphia.

This special room, bright and cheerful with colorful pillows and posters, is off limits to adults, including the faculty member who is the supervisor of the project. She is available for consultation but she remains outside the Unwinding Room. This room is for the troubled student and her peers who have been trained to help her, including one experienced counselor who is always present when any girl needs help.

The experienced peer counselors who staff the Unwinding Room have received about two hundred hours of training spread over a one-year period. They attend orientation sessions at Philadelphia's Temple University and in-service training courses conducted by the Diagnostic Rehabilitation Center. Through their training they become familiar with techniques of peer counseling, techniques of group dynamics, problems of self-identity, and facts about drugs and the motivations to use drugs. While the drug problem appears to be less prevalent at Saint Maria Goretti than it is in a number of other high schools, the peer counselors are prepared to provide help if a problem or potential problem appears.

A student may come to the Unwinding Room for any problem that is troubling her—she can't get along with her mother; she feels the people she would like to have as friends don't like her; she thinks she wants to drop out of school; or she needs to talk about some vague, undefined problem.

The trained teen counselor and any other staff members who are present respond to the need of their troubled colleague. They listen as she describes her problem, helping her make it explicit by asking questions until the difficulty becomes clear to them. Discussing her problem at length often helps a student see the problem more clearly herself and sometimes leads to a redefinition of what the problem was originally perceived to be.

Once a problem is clearly defined, solutions are sought. Role playing is used to dramatize the difficulty and to help the troubled girl see the problem from the viewpoints of several people. Discussion follows the role playing, and suggestions for action are made.

The Unwinding Room operates without any special funding. Its resources are the peer counselors, ranging in number from ten to twenty, one adult supervisor and a supportive faculty, and the personnel who train the counselors. As the supervisor points out, some of the problems discussed in the special center might seem to be trivial, but to the troubled teen girl, "they appear to be huge, intolerable, serious. What seems especially welcome is an opportunity to talk about them privately . . . with persons who are of the same age, persons who are sympathetic, persons who are of the same culture and have much the same values."

POLITICAL ACTION PROGRAMS

CLAY COUNTY YOUTH ORGANIZATION
CLAY COUNTY, MISSISSIPPI

In the early 1960s the civil rights movement came to Mississippi. Slowly the poverty-stricken black communities of the state became alive with new ideas and activity. SNCC and the freedom schools came to West Point in Clay County, and out of these programs arose not only a new consciousness that something could be done to improve the lot of Mississippi blacks, but also a new generation of young boys and girls dedicated to achieving that improvement. From an early age —in many cases as young as twelve and thirteen—the black young people of West Point had a clear, hard, realistic vision of the forces that oppressed them and of the forces that might liberate them. Even after the freedom schools departed, a group of these young people met regularly at the Ebony Lounge to discuss their plans, their aspirations, and their common experiences. In 1968 they founded the Ebony Lounge Youth Organization, which later became the Clay County Youth Organization (CCYO).

CCYO has about forty active members, all of whom are or have recently been students at West Point's Fifth Street Senior High School. Any young person in Clay County can join. The organization holds regular meetings in a building that the members themselves renovated. The group tries to be informal in structure, but there are officers and an executive board, and there are by-laws to be followed. Many of the organization's present officers began, before they were even teenagers, by working with the early freedom schools. The organization has an adult advisor who is also Director of the Clay County Community Development Organization, a community action organization that sponsors CCYO. He has great confidence in the young people and encourages them to exercise initiative and take on responsibility.

In discussing the Youth Advocates program earlier, much was said about the gap between youth problems and the resources that the adult community has available for dealing with them. It is important to note that this gap is as prevalent in the black communities of the southern states as it is in any other community in the nation. Generalizations are hazardous, but it might at least be said that the older blacks in the South tend to be conservative and relatively content or at least "accepting"; the young people tend to be progressive and discontented. But if the young people are to be effectively active, they must take into account the total community setting and work within the framework of the black community as a whole in their efforts to help their peers. Thus, while it is true that some of the lay County Youth Organization's projects have been aimed very specifically at youth problems (for example, the group organized a walk-out at Fifth Street Senior High School to demand better heating, better books, and better teachers, and they have, with some success, made requests for more public recreational facilities), their most successful contributions to the welfare of their peers have come through activities that have been planned with the whole black community in mind.

The Youth Organization, for instance, has been instrumental in the successful voter registration drives in Clay County; today between eighty and ninety percent of the eligible blacks in the County are registered to vote. It also operates a much needed day care center.

Perhaps most impressive of all, CCYO ran a successful boycott of white West Point business establishments. The circumstances surrounding this boycott illustrate the extremely serious and demanding situations members of the Clay County Youth Organization face in their everyday lives. A few years ago, the man who is now the CCYO's advisor ran for mayor of West Point. One day while he was campaigning, a group of whites drove up to his sound truck and shot the driver, wounding him fatally. In response to this killing, CCYO, in cooperation with its sponsor, the Clay County Community Development Organization, organized a boycott of West Point's white-owned businesses. In a list of demands published on September 29, 1970, the black community demanded the conviction of the killer, the end of police brutality, the appointment of blacks to a civilian police review board, increased employment of blacks in shops and public offices, free transportation for children who live more than a mile from school, the elimination of split school sessions, the appointment of blacks to the Board of Education, the development of public recreational facilities, and a Model Cities program. The boycott lasted for ten months and forced several businesses into bankruptcy. One result of the closing of some white-owned markets was the construction of a new black-owned supermarket in West Point. Several of the boycott demands, including improvements in the police department and in town recreational facilities, have been met.

An examination of the Youth Organization's relationship with the Clay County Community Development Organization in this boycott and with the black community as a whole leads to the conclusion that the Youth Organization was the organizing force, the true leader. This preeminent role has carried over into other activities as well. Members of the Youth Organization serve on the Board of Directors of the Clay County Community Development Organization, although no CCCDO adults serve on the Youth Organization's Board.

The Organization's Director knows, as does most of the West Point community, that the Clay County Youth Organization is composed of mature, realistic, experienced young people who can be counted on for imaginative planning and for follow-through. These young people, who have spent seven or eight years struggling for equal rights and opportunities, have learned that the coming years will call for dedication to hard, practical gains in the fields of politics, education, and economics.

The CCYO has virtually no operating money. Some of its leaders have participated in training programs funded by foundation grants, but no money comes directly into West Point for the organization's use. Because the black community in West Point is poor, local contributions are inevitably small. But the Youth Organization manages to maintain its own house, and its many members continue to participate enthusiastically in a variety of activities. For the present, manpower seems to be an adequate substitute for lack of funds, and the program shows that a youth organization can be of inestimable help to a community, even without many dollars to support it.

YOUTH CITIZENSHIP FUND, INC.
WASHINGTON, D.C.

The Clay County Youth Organization is one illustration of young people becoming involved in political action on a community level, as one part of its overall program. Another illustration of youth involvement in political action is to be found in a Washington, D.C., project whose major focus is on electoral reform and on stimulating young people to take an active part in the political process.

Youth Citizenship Fund, Inc. (YCF) is a Washington-based organization of young people who are concerned about voter registration and electoral reform and whose objective is to increase youth participation in the political system. The formation of the organization, in September 1970, was prompted by reports of the apathetic attitude of youth toward voting and toward exercising the political influence they could have. In 1968, for example, in states where eighteen to twenty year olds were eligible to vote, only thirty-three and three tenths percent cast a ballot.

The group, with a paid staff of eleven young people, mainly of college age, and a large number of youth volunteers has focused on three major programs:

1.   Citizenship Education. This includes research and reports on the location, hours, and forms to be filled out at the polls; development and testing of curriculum and techniques to stimulate political awareness and provide practical know-how on voter registration and on running for office; and a Youth Internship Program that enables ten outstanding political science students to receive college credit for spending eight

weeks during the summer researching, lobbying, and reporting on national issues of their choice.

2. Research on Uniform Voting Procedures Act. Concerned by the absence of uniformity in voter registration requirements, YCF has worked to develop a uniform set of principles for state-by-state adoption or enactment by Congress. The program has involved research into existing state laws and the development of kits and manuals that outline advantageous voter registration requirements and suggest ways to achieve them on local, state, and national levels.

3. Voter Participation. To increase political participation, YCF provides technical aid and information to existing groups engaged in promoting voter participation and registration. Professional consultants assist with organization, fund raising, implementation, and evaluations.

This young, politically conscious group has conducted two pilot voter registration drives—one in Chicago and the other in Washington, D.C. In Chicago the drive brought in between thirty-five and forty-five thousand new eighteen- to twenty-year-old registrants; in Washington, more than fifty-four thousand five hundred new voters were registered. Other such drives have been initiated—one in Kentucky and another in Massachusetts.

Most of the participants in YCF are college students or young people of college age, but there is support from many adults, and there is also a continuing effort to involve high school students. For example, YCF conducts training programs to prepare high school students to work with their peers and their teachers to provide information to students and to stimulate interest in political action. In some instances, college students involved in YCF have made arrangements to go to high schools to talk with students and faculty about the need for political awareness and about ways to stimulate it.

YCF activities are planned and implemented by youth, with the assistance of legal counsel and of a Board of Directors composed of adults from such national organizations as the United Steelworkers of America, Common Cause, and the League of Women Voters. The approach of the organization has been youth-talking-to-youth in a direct nonpartisan appeal for participation in the political system. YCF believes that any effective method of interesting young people in the political process must originate with young people and must include the recognition that youth is capable of providing ideas and leadership for political reform and social change.

JUVENILE DELINQUENCY PROGRAMS

CALIFORNIA YOUTH AUTHORITY,
O. H. CLOSE SCHOOL STUDENT AIDE PROGRAM
STOCKTON, CALIFORNIA

It has been a commonly held assumption that the impact of older delinquents on younger delinquents is nearly always injurious. Hundreds of superintendents and wardens of institutions for juvenile offenders would say that this has been borne out by their experience; because of conditions existing in their institutions, this has no doubt been the case.

But at least one institution in California has tried something quite different. Embracing the helper therapy principle discussed in the section on Youth Tutoring Youth programs in chapter 3, the O. H. Close School in Stockton, California (a facility of the California Youth Authority) has adopted a program in which carefully selected older delinquents act as tutors, counselors, and recreational leaders for younger delinquents. The program, funded under Title I of ESEA, has been very successful.

In October 1967, the California Youth Authority began selecting young men for the Student Aide Project. The Authority selected young men who had been committed by the courts to its Youth Training School in Ontario, California, an institution for older offenders. To be eligible for selection, the young men were to be between eighteen and twenty-two years old and have completed at least nine years of academic schooling. Furthermore, they must not have committed certain specified kinds of violent crimes.

The first group, fifteen in number, arrived at the O. H. Close School in January 1968, to begin work with younger wards. Today, the program maintains between forty and forty-five Student Aides divided into groups of no more than fifteen. Each group of Aides spends nine months in the program. The first two months are devoted to screening and selection at the Youth Training School (the rate of attrition averages between thirty and fifty percent). Any youth who expresses an interest in the program is interviewed by a Student Aide Coordinator. If he appears to be a possible candidate, he is subjected to a full selections procedure in which the program requirements outlined above, test results, and character appraisals are all considered. During the third month, candidates undergo an orientation program at the Youth Training School. This provides them with approximately sixty hours of background about the jobs they are to undertake and gives them an opportunity to decide whether they really want to participate in the program.

At the beginning of the fourth month, the candidates who have weathered the selection procedures are sent to the O. H. Close School where they are given another sixty hours of training in very specific techniques of recreation, counseling, and tutoring. They are also given on-the-job training and introduced to the daily routine of being a Student Aide. Periodic meetings are held to discuss the Aides' progress. At the beginning of the fifth month, each new Aide is assigned to a unit; the assignment is made in terms of the Aide's abilities and preferences. For the rest of his time in the program, the Aide serves in this unit—a unit that has responsibility for a specific set of tasks or a specific set of younger wards.

A typical day for a Student Aide might consist of tutoring

or helping in the reading lab until noon, eating lunch and having some free time until mid-afternoon, studying or undergoing treatment of his own problems from 3 p.m. until 6 p.m., and helping with recreation or counseling after dinner. If he has not completed high school, the Aide must also devote time to his own academic program. All the Student Aides live in their own special dormitory at the Close School; this dormitory is separate from the dormitories of the younger wards.

The functions of the Student Aides might be summarized as follows: providing formal assistance through tutoring, counseling, and recreation; providing informal assistance through serving as role models for the younger wards; and providing formal and informal assistance as mediators and as interpreters of differences between the value systems of wards coming from youth subcultures and those of the middle-class-oriented California Youth Authority staff.

After completing the nine-month program, most Aides are paroled and about forty-five percent are placed in paraprofessional social service jobs. A very important part of the program is that it prepares Aides not only to help younger wards, but also to perform social service jobs generally as preparation for further academic training in the social service field. The helper role that is the backbone of the program is strengthened by the conviction that most Aides gain experience and skills that will lead to a related career in the community.

The relationship between the younger wards and the older Aides has been remarkably fruitful. In their study on *Delinquency and Opportunity*,[2] Cloward and Ohlin noted how age status influences the transmission of delinquent behavior patterns and values; in gangs that have senior, junior, and midget divisions, the younger members model themselves on the

2. Richard A. Cloward and Lloyd E. Ohlin. *Delinquency and Opportunity: A Theory of Delinquent Gangs.* New York: Free Press, 1960.

older gang members. At O. H. Close School, this influence on the learning process is utilized to convey acceptable, law-abiding standards of behavior instead of delinquent standards. "Most of the kids don't want to appear childish when the Aides are around. They act a little more mature in their presence and try to copy them in their work," one staff member at Close commented.

Another staff member, a unit counselor, observed that in his unit of mostly low-maturity wards, "When one boy gets excited, the rest seem to pick it up; now we're seeing fewer boys involved in acting-out incidents. The younger boys seem to look forward to be [sic] this age—I only hope they don't think they can eventually also become aides."

Still another staff member has testified: "What did we expect initially? Anything from manipulation to homosexuality. Certainly at the beginning some of the Aides tended to identify more with the wards than with the staff. But I am impressed by the way each of the Aides seems to have a special talent. One has an art class with seven kids. He keeps them interested and sets a good example. Another Aide is particularly good in woodwork and is a tremendous asset to the boys in the shop."

The Student Aide Project has, of course, encountered problems, and adjustments continue to be made. During the program's initial months of operation, there was much concern over defining the role of the Aide. He was to be something more than a ward, yet something less than staff; he was considered by many younger wards as staff, yet he had none of the authority of staff; he could counsel and lead, but he could not discipline. These ambiguities often confused the Aides themselves. After the first few months, it became apparent that more attention to the Aides' personal problems would have to be offered—more than was originally anticipated.

At one point, the Project was modified to see what might happen if Aides selected from nearby detention centers were brought directly to the Close School without being required to spend any time at all in the Youth Training School. After a short period of operation on this basis, it was discovered that new Aides showed less dedication to their positions than the Aides from the Youth Training School had shown. Becoming an Aide had seemed to be too "easy" for many of these new boys; they hadn't developed sufficient respect for their new roles nor sufficient knowledge of the complexity of their work. After this unsuccessful effort, the Project went back to taking only boys from the Youth Training School.

More recently the proliferation of interesting programs developed for its young people by the California Youth Authority has made it difficult for the Student Aide Project to recruit enough high caliber people. It is still popular and its participants are full of praise for it, but competition among programs to attract the best applicants is now stiff.

When the talent has been available, the Student Aide Project has worked admirably well. Since the program's beginning, one hundred and fifty young men have participated in it; of these, only twenty-seven have quit or have been asked to leave. Seventy of the program's graduates have been released on parole; of these, only eight have had their parole revoked —an incredibly low rate of recidivism for the California Youth Authority. According to a recent survey, all the program's released graduates are employed or attending college.

For the future, the program's coordinator has at least two improvements in mind. First, he would like to see the Aides housed in an off-campus building so they can be free of the feeling that they are on the job twenty-four hours a day. It would be much better for the Aides, he feels, if they could think of their positions just as they would think of any regular job in the outside world. Second, he would like to see the surrounding Stockton community make better use of the valuable resource that these O. H. Close Aides represent. He points to racial disturbances in the Stockton schools and suggests that the Aides, trained to act freely and easily in a completely integrated environment and familiar with the psychological factors that can lead to disruptive and illegal acts, could contribute to the resolution of such problems.

This last possibility seems to suggest ways in which programs such as the Student Aide Project at O. H. Close could be of use to schools in many communities. In addition, it leads to speculation that the need to place youngsters in detention facilities might well be obviated if the public schools, acting in conjunction with juvenile court authorities, developed programs involving use of the helper therapy principle.

SURROUND
RED WING, MINNESOTA

Still another possible relationship between schools and delinquents is suggested by the SURROUND program operated by the Protestant chaplain at the State Training School, Red Wing, Minnesota. SURROUND organizes groups of girls and boys from more than two hundred churches in Minnesota and brings them to the Red Wing State Training School where they are expected to "surround" individual delinquent boys with positive peer culture experiences. Five to ten church youths usually meet with one delinquent for recreation and for discussion. (The contacts made at Red Wing are often continued once the delinquent youth returns to his home.) In addition, SURROUND members try to educate their own communities about delinquency and about the kinds of growth that are achieved at the Training School: The purpose here is to increase community acceptance of returning delinquents.

There is much more that can be done for juvenile delinquents than is now being done. The Student Aide Program and SURROUND are only suggestive of a great range of programs that might be developed to allow a juvenile delinquent to feel more a part of a healthy, responsible society and thereby free himself from his delinquency. The idea that these and comparable programs promote is that young people—delinquents and nondelinquents alike—can contribute substantially to the rehabilitation of young people.

A FURTHER WORD

This chapter has described situations in which young people have become resources for whole groups of young people, whole youth communities. But it is important to observe that these responses to youth problems, while very impressive, are not the only responses that young people have developed. For each problem, young people respond in a wide variety of ways. It is perhaps this variety, representing the ingenuity of youth, that should be stressed more than any other quality. For instance, in dealing with the problems of drugs and runaways, HELP in Philadelphia and Youth to Youth on Drug Abuse Education in San Francisco have each developed approaches quite distinct from one another and distinct also from the approach taken by Youth Advocates in Seattle.

It is probably true that today's young people, who each year seem to mature a little earlier, face a greater number of severe personal problems than their predecessors—and at an earlier age. But it is reassuring to observe that the same forces that have helped to produce these severe problems seem also to have produced young people who are better able to solve their problems.

All the projects described in this chapter are examples of what young people can do. The resources youth have are genuinely needed by society, and they deserve the respect and support of the adult community.

now what?

Here, everything is measured by status symbols: the biggest, the most. There's a lot of fighting and grabbing for the buck. . . . Now, we're getting more people working for something outside themselves, for the betterment of mankind and society. What we're doing is refusing the short-term gains of status and gratification. The gains we are fighting for are long-term and involve living for others, some of whom are not yet born.

You see, part of what we've got to do is help ourselves. Adults always have had the authority, and now kids don't know what to do even when they have the chance. So, we've got to learn what to do and how to do it. . . . The thing is, now we're getting some say in things, **some authority, and we now know what to do with it to bring about constructive change.**

The projects described in the preceding seven chapters cover a broad range of youth activities. Some are service-oriented; some focus on arts, crafts, and trades; some combine service functions with other activities such as communications and teaching. And there are scores more—in Maine, students are helping preserve national forests; in Coos Bay, Oregon, they are finding ruptures in city sewage mains and are preventing pollution of the waterfront. Throughout the country, more and more teenagers are becoming involved in and committed to projects that better their communities.

The "brand name" for this kind of project varies. Some educators call it "participatory education," others call it "experiential" or "action learning." In fact, this type of learning experience thrives in numerous schools without any label. But in all youth projects, the principle is the same—young people learn by doing, provided the doing demands decision-making and active participation.

For specific information about how these kinds of projects are developed, case histories are the most informative. Realistically and practically, questions about initiating and maintaining a project have to be answered with reference to the local setting and existing participants—youth and adults.

With this in mind, there are still some general principles that can apply to a variety of projects. This final chapter provides a few suggestions that may be helpful for adults —teachers, church workers, or personnel in youth service agencies—who are interested in developing projects that will enhance the learning of young people, contribute to their feelings of personal worth and self-esteem, and, at the same time, provide benefits for others.

The suggestions are organized around the following questions: (1) What are good youth participation projects? (2) How have some started? (3) What characterizes an effective adult leader? (4) What are some of the steps in starting and operating projects?

CHARACTERISTICS OF "GOOD" YOUTH PARTICIPATION PROJECTS

This book illustrates that there can be many kinds of youth participation projects. Some involve only poor youth; others include youth from all socio-economic backgrounds. Some concern only a few youth; others many. Some are operated entirely by young people; others by youth who work collaboratively with adults. Some call for full- or part-time work for a semester, a few weeks, or just a few hours. Some provide paid work, although most provide for non-paid volunteer service only. Some operate as part of ongoing programs in schools and youth-serving or other social agencies; others function outside established institutions.

While these operational characteristics differ widely, good projects have one overriding characteristic—they offer a young person a type of participation that demands responsible action on his part, provides him opportunities to make decisions that affect himself and others, and lets him experience the consequences of his own action and decisions. Good projects also have a common goal—they all aim to help young people grow, achieve, and develop positive attitudes toward themselves as participants in the adult world.

Since our culture offers so few opportunities for initiating young people into adulthood and its responsibilities, it is imperative that those who plan to launch youth participation programs make sure they meet these objectives. Some criteria are needed as guides to help analyze whether a proposed project meets these objectives and will be a good one.

One way to establish criteria is to identify characteristics found in better programs. This is one procedure the National Commission on Resources for Youth, Inc., uses in reviewing projects to determine which ones merit the attention of other people. The following list of characteristics draws upon guidelines published elsewhere by the Commission and incorporates suggestions from consultants and collaborating youth participation project directors.

The project must be responsive to the needs of the young people involved. Youth participation means that young people's interests and skills should shape the style and direction of programs. This is especially true for youth in their teens. Their greatest need at this transitional stage is an opportunity to develop the skills and attitudes that will ease their maturation into adulthood. Maturity is promoted by providing active roles in planning, developing, and operating projects. Young people who participate in decision-making and actively follow through on their decisions develop a sense of proprietorship and pride in their work. Furthermore, they experience the excitement that comes from knowing that their own actions are affecting individuals with whom they work and, perhaps, even the agencies or institutions where they work. This can generate enthusiasm and commitment—both important to young people during their adolescent years.

A young person also needs to be challenged. This challenge should be suitable to both his age and abilities and at the same time stretch his intellectual and emotional capacities. It should provide an opportunity to do something that is both meaningful and difficult—difficult in the sense that it requires him to reach beyond his previous range of knowledge or performance. Meeting such a challenge can lead a young person to reappraise his expectations of his own achievements and ultimately to value his own abilities. This results in enhanced self-concept.

By permitting youth a working partnership with adults, good projects can help meet another youth need—that of a supportive adult role model. This partnership occurs where there is mutuality in teaching and learning and where each age group sees its importance as a resource for the other and offers what it uniquely can provide.

As they approach the responsibilities of adulthood, a very

practical need of youth is to explore the options available in the real world of work. A good youth participation project, therefore, offers exposure to work opportunities that touch careers in the trades, services, and professions. Young people can test their interests and potential through work assignments in several of these areas. They can become familiar with the training required for each of them and thus be better prepared to make an informed choice of their future careers.

Finally, we know that during adolescence particularly, youth have a need to feel that they belong and are accepted by peers and adults whom they respect. Unfortunately, many facets of today's life—broken homes, small family size, frequent relocation of families, crowded schools, and frequent change of schools—contribute to a sense of alienation and isolation on the part of young people. A good youth participation project can counteract this. It offers a young person an opportunity to belong to a group working for a common goal, experiencing the satisfaction and exhilaration that comes from being associated with others in significant work. Joint accomplishments and learning by students and teachers contribute directly to a sense of community.

The project must be responsive to genuine needs of the community. It is important that youth participating in projects have work assignments that are recognized as important and necessary. The work activity must be real. It should not be "made work" designed to keep young people occupied or just "do gooding." Ideally, the work should focus on some crucial community problem (health, drugs, environment, and the like) that young people can help alleviate through their service. It is essential that the work be respected by youth, their peers, and the community. Adult respect for the work must be evidenced concretely. It might, for example, be accepted as part of the school curriculum, carrying credit, or, when appropriate, carry financial remuneration.

The project must provide a learning experience for the

young people involved in it. It is a mistake to assume that work by itself will generate an educational experience, but a good youth participation project always uses the work aspect as a basis for learning. Students are encouraged to examine themselves in action, to reflect on their experiences, analyze the problems connected with them, and digest their thinking. In group discussions where young people share these impressions with each other and a supportive adult, they make the learning their own. They may, as a result, generate and try out different ways of working on the job or different attitudes toward the job. Their discussions may develop some theoretical understanding of how the work relates to the problems and needs of the community. They also serve as a self-correcting mechanism for the program and should be built into all projects to insure ongoing evaluation, feedback, and accountability. Adults who are natural youth leaders will know instinctively how to facilitate discussions. Others may find that some training in group communications is helpful. Whether this skill is innate or acquired, it is essential that adults know how to use it to enhance youths' learning.

Youth participation projects can often be part of the traditional school curriculum, and the school should integrate the experiential learning into its regular school program. In this way, the curriculum can relate theory to practice, thus facilitating more learning to guide further practice.

For some projects it may be necessary to provide skill training if the work demands special competencies. In most projects such training is given by the receiving agency that enjoys the benefits of youth services. Where possible this training, too, should be related to the school curriculum.

The learning that takes place in youth participation projects ideally goes beyond the acquisition of academic knowledge or the mastering of a skill. It should include personal growth as well. Since most youth engaged in these projects are adolescents, it is important that the learning foster a growth process that encourages them to discover themselves in relation to their environment, to find their identity, and to begin to build a firm sense of self. Experiential learning growing out of first-hand experience is a natural vehicle for such growth. Project directors report that as skills increase and insights deepen, they detect a basic revision in the way adolescents view themselves, their teachers, and the persons with whom they work.

The many learning possibilities inherent in youth participation projects need to be researched. Observation of ongoing projects over a period of time indicates that the good programs —those where the work experience provides genuine responsibility and an opportunity for real interaction with other people of different ages—have powerful educational results. They almost seem to be providing a new method of socializing young people.

HOW SOME PROJECTS HAVE STARTED

Most successful youth projects are initiated in response to an unmet need identified by young people, by their teachers or principals, or by community agencies. An example of a successful project initiated by young people themselves is the Student Coalition for Relevant Sex Education in New York City described in the chapter on Youth as Curriculum Builders. The program began in 1971 when a group of students formed a coalition to convince the Board of Education of the need for a relevant program of sex education. They collected signatures on a petition and wrote a proposal for the project with the help of the staff of Planned Parenthood. The Planned Parenthood organization also donated office space, a telephone, and help in managing finances.

The first petition, with 8,000 signatures, was lost by the Board of Education. Undaunted, the students collected fresh signatures. In the meetings that followed, the proposal was endorsed by Board members, and prompt action was promised. Soon after, the schools' Chancellor officially requested project support from city high schools and received it.

As a result of the long struggle by these students, peer counselors in New York City schools now provide referral services and information on sex problems, such as pregnancy and venereal disease, that concern adolescents. Rap rooms have been established, and the faculty in a number of schools have helped the students establish elective, credited courses on human sexuality.

Another project, the Social Studies Laboratory in Enfield, Connecticut, described in the chapter on Youth as Curriculum Builders, was initiated largely by one student.

A community survey conducted by youth has often been followed by youthful action to alleviate local problems. For example, this occurred in Action Community, a project in Detroit, Michigan, described in the chapter on Youth as Community Problem-Solvers. Students collected photos and interviews documenting unsafe housing, poor recreational facilities, class differences, and youth unemployment. Based on their analysis of the most serious community problems, the students then formed interest groups. Each group studied its chosen problem more deeply and began to formulate solutions. The housing group again used cameras to implement the next phase of their work. They created a slide presentation to inform residents of the loans available to use in rehabilitating their homes. The recreational group surveyed attitudes about local needs and then enlisted the help of a professional planner to design new facilities.

These are but three of many instances where youth involvement in curriculum changes or in providing community service originated with young people themselves. Sometimes student interest can be sparked by a teacher who provides information about other youth projects. Information about ongoing projects can come from newspapers, magazine articles, or from *New Roles for Youth in the School and the Community.*

Sometimes a principal, teacher, or group of teachers may take the initiative more directly and provide the impetus for the development of youth participation activities. For example, a sensitive faculty may respond to students' apathy toward school as evidenced by their truancy and dropping out. The many high school business enterprises at Manual High School in Denver, described in the chapter on Youth as Entrepreneurs, reflect the inventiveness and continuing support of the principal and a number of the teachers and their attempt to transform the students' school.

Still other programs have been initiated by a community agency, as was the case in the Teenage Tenant Training Council, described in the chapter on Youth as Community Problem-Solvers. This project developed when a settlement house worker suggested that the young people of the neighborhood provide assistance in solving a serious housing problem in an area of New York City where deteriorating tenements were occupied by poor, non-English-speaking people who knew nothing of their rights as tenants. A wise adult leader helped design the program so that the youths' work involved more than the drudgery of inspection and repetitive tasks. The program provided the opportunity for the young men to study housing laws, examine the operation of a large city department charged with enforcing them, and to explore, try out, and redesign techniques in group orientation. The teenagers acquired valuable skills, experienced personal satisfaction, and were able to earn money through funds made available for the project.

The important point in all these projects is that the young people fully recognized the importance of a particular problem or need and subsequently developed proposals for action. There are limitless variations for potential projects. The opportunities for projects are so great that they warrant setting up an Office of Student Involvement in every high school to research the community's needs and to arrange for student placement. One model for such a bureau, which is staffed by students with faculty serving as advisors, is operating in some schools participating in the Student-Community Involvement Project in Minneapolis, Minnesota.

Discovering unmet needs is not difficult. As students become more comfortable with the adults they work with, they will openly express their gripes and complaints about things needed around the school or in the community, and this can trigger a demand for immediate action. It then becomes the task of the adults to help the students analyze all facets of the contemplated work and to help fix priorities for action.

CHARACTERISTICS OF AN EFFECTIVE ADULT LEADER

Since this book is addressed mainly to adults, particularly educators, and since the presence of supportive adults has consistently proved to be a crucial factor in almost all successful youth participation projects, the adult leader deserves special attention. A supportive adult working with young people makes a major contribution through his own attitudes about youth and their capabilities.

An examination of almost any successful project will show that the adults involved themselves not as teachers or project directors, but rather as facilitators, to help the young people achieve *their* goals. Adults who can precipitate youthful decision-making without controlling it are a special breed, and wise administrators will spot them and enlist their efforts on behalf of young people.

A prevalent misconception among adults who work with teenage youth is that they themselves must act like teenagers. This is a particularly misleading notion for adults who work in programs of youth participation—young people need adult models. They need to work with adults who take themselves seriously as adults. Likewise, they need adults who take young people seriously—who believe in the capacity of young people. These characteristics, rather than "personality," "popularity," or "charisma," make for effective adult supervision. For example, one very successful youth program is led by an irascible, short-tempered man who shouts at the young people and interrupts them mid-sentence, while another is run by a soft-spoken woman who is hardly older than her students and who is not Puerto Rican, although the project is located in a Puerto Rican community. The manners of these adults could not be more different, yet underlying the gruff orders or the quiet smile is the same affirmation of self and belief in the young people. And the young people respond; they want to take their adult leaders seriously, just as they want to be taken seriously themselves. This requires adult integrity and a certain frankness about who they are, what they can do, and what they believe young people can do.

To activate latent qualities of leadership and commitment in young people, it is important that adults give precedence to individual development over other project results. But this priority doesn't preclude adults from an emotional commitment to the concrete goals of the project itself. Students and adults who are partners in pursuit of a single goal become increasingly able to share their feelings about their work, about themselves, and about each other. Often, working together with a shared goal brings even the most disparate group of individuals together and creates a sense of community, all too unusual today.

In youth participation projects, young people find themselves in circumstances that press them to discover and use their own resourcefulness and reliability. These opportunities are a natural result of mutually-run projects in which adults have an enduring faith in the capability of their students, an unfailing sensitivity to their needs, and an honest acceptance of the interdependence between themselves and the young people.

When this climate of mutual acceptance permeates the atmosphere in which the adults and young people are working, strong feelings and concerns are bound to emerge. A sensitive adult leader will *seize the moment* to help move students toward action. This was poignantly illustrated in the way in which skilled teachers of a public alternative high school in San Francisco dealt with their students' concern over the death of a fellow student as a result of an overdose of a large quantity of depressants:

The deceased girl's classmates were initially encouraged to try to verbalize their grief and shock. Once this happened, they were very much at odds, they didn't seem able to leave each other, nor did they seem able to stay where they were. They were quietly asked to think about what they were wishing in regard to the situation. One student shyly said that he was wishing the impossible—that their dead sister would return. However, if that could not happen, the next wish was almost as impossible —that others would remember their grief and themselves begin to change. He wanted to "take every friend he knew and himself as well, shake everyone to the roots and get them to stop using drugs." Many others in the room nodded agreement, they felt some sort of mission to get the word out to other kids. At that point, one of the adults suggested that they sit with those feelings for a day and return with any ideas they might have for realizing their vision for helping themselves and others like themselves in this important area.

The next day, after a good deal of discussion, two concrete projects emerged. First, the students decided to organize a rock benefit to collect enough money to pay part of the funeral expenses of their deceased classmate. Next, they decided to work on a drug publication, which would be dedicated to their classmate and designed to help others like themselves; they later called this pamphlet *Don't Die in Vein*. Thus, the students mobilized their deep feelings and energy in a manner which was especially meaningful for them.

MAJOR STEPS IN STARTING
AND OPERATING PROJECTS

The young people who will participate in a program should be involved in some way in all the steps required for its initiation and development. Not only does this involvement give them a sense of their own responsibility for the program, it also lets them learn how to evaluate ideas and plans, how to develop a detailed plan for action, and how to follow through on that plan.

This requires the adult to be receptive to ideas of young people. No matter how farfetched a scheme may seem to the adult, the fact that a young person has thought seriously enough about a project to present it is in itself important. By permitting students to imagine freely, to explore, and then to analyze, the adult is encouraging learning.

If students are accustomed to doing what is expected of them, refraining from expressing judgments or making suggestions, a more open climate must be created. The adult needs to provide assurance that ideas and feelings, negative as well as positive, can be expressed and received in a nonjudgmental atmosphere. To encourage students to express ideas and opinions, especially at the beginning of a project, it may be helpful to use some techniques that provide for anonymity, such as encouraging written, unsigned suggestions or criticisms.

In general, however, young people are eager to find worthy outlets for their abundant energies. The most exciting kinds of programs emerge from a felt need that the students themselves express. For example, they might be verbalizing discontent about a situation in the school or community. A responsive adult can help them delineate their dissatisfactions. He or she might encourage them to fantasize an ideal solution. It is important that students be allowed to let themselves go during these brainstorming sessions; in the developmental stage, nothing is too far out. Adults need to encourage young people to dream about what they can be and do. A wise leader will then help them return to reality and begin to focus on one manageable area of their concern where they can have some impact. The final stages in starting a program involve concrete planning and then beginning.

The real trick in this kind of project is to capitalize on youth's spontaneity and guide it to constructive action. One teacher described this process:

Our kids were griping that they weren't studying anything that was meaningful to them, that their courses were boring, and that they still had trouble reading. Rather than defensively telling them that they were not working hard enough, we tried to get them to surface their dissatisfactions and encouraged them to fantasize the ideal situation. Only when the idea had been thoroughly explored did we suggest that they focus on a solution. They decided to initiate a program of teaching reading to young children because someone in the group suggested that one learns by teaching, and they felt this program would improve their own reading skills. Once this became the focus of their project, they were able to mobilize their energies around starting and operating the project.

When students' reactions to a proposed project are mixed, with only a few showing interest, then the entire group should not be involved. In an open climate, youth are free to consider various options and select from among them. It is axiomatic that only those interested should participate in a project.

When students become interested and begin raising questions themselves, an activity is off to a good start. If this doesn't happen, the adult needs to be ready with a few questions, for example: What do you think about this project? Do you think it is worthwhile? Why or why not? *Why* should such a project be started? *How* might it get started? If you were living in that community, would you like to take part in that activity? What would you like to do? Why? What would you expect to get out of it? If this project were introduced into our curriculum, do you think it would make school more interesting? If so, why?

At this point, students need to look beyond their personal interests in the activity and explore further reasons for proceeding. Interest is one good criterion for deciding to undertake a project, but interest alone won't provide the guidance needed for its actual development.

While batting around ideas, students can eliminate some program possibilities, if a few key questions are raised. When students do not bring these up themselves, the adult might present such queries as: Do you consider this program really important? Is it important to other young people as well as yourselves? Can you assume a significant role in charting its directions, or will you have to depend solely on adults? Is this being done someplace else in the school—or the community—and better? (After this question, one might suggest a halt to investigate and track down this information.) Will doing this project be a challenge to you or give you any skills and/or experience you'd like to have? Do you think you can learn from it? Can you keep it going long enough to make a dent, or at least to see if you can accomplish what you set out to do? How long will it take? Do you think this is something another group could pick up, once you have shown the way?

By spending time on planning at the beginning of a program, students will be able to move more easily into action and will have done the groundwork to assure support from the involved adults. It would be advisable at this point to develop a statement of goals and purposes to be sure that everyone (be it two or two hundred students) agrees with and understands the objectives of the project. After that, questions such as the following need to be answered and included in a written plan students themselves develop:

What will we be doing? How much time will it take? What about the scheduling? What will our hours be? If it's a school program, can we work during school hours? If we work after school hours, can we receive credit?

How many people will it take to run it? How many students? How many adults? Who will be in charge of the project? Who does what?

Do we need support from the school? What kind? Do we need permission to leave the campus?

Does the project represent enough change from the accustomed school program that parents need early information about what is being planned? If so, how can this information be made available to them? How can we help in this step? Are there ways parents can help, beyond the acceptance of the worth of the project and a supportive attitude? Do we need permission from our parents to participate? Is there a form to sign?

Are there any legal obstacles to carrying out the project? Do we have to be covered by insurance? If so, who provides insurance—the school, the place where we work, our parents? Do we have to be a certain age to participate? Do we need work permits? If so, how do we get them?

If transportation to the work site is needed, who will provide it? The school? Public transportation? Our own cars? Who will cover the cost of car expenses, including insurance?

What kinds of materials and equipment do we need for the project? Are these available at the school? Can we make our own?

Do we need money to finance the project? Is it available through school budgeted funds? If not, where might it be obtained? How much is needed? Can we reduce the amount needed and still have a good project?

These questions are not intended as an all inclusive how-to list of suggestions. They are intended simply as starting points and may include questions that apply only to some projects. Each project has its own set of requirements that students and adults need to identify, and each project will undoubtedly generate other questions. The bibliography, (see page 243) contains references to several excellent publications that outline many commendable how-to procedures.

The major assistance adults can give during this process is to help young people locate sources of information. It is especially important that the adults be familiar with the wide variety of community resources to which the young people can turn for information and advice. And, although it is important to encourage youth to do what they can with limited resources, it is helpful if the adult has some information about funding sources. Money is often an essential ingredient in getting programs started, and if the school, church, or community agency is serious about encouraging a program, the adult staff does have some responsibility to help students explore the funding resources the school or agency has or may acquire. This is particularly important in situations where minors cannot themselves be recipients of grants, as is the case with most federal, state, or foundation funding.

Almost always it will be necessary to secure acceptance of a program from the school or agency that has jurisdiction over the students. Ideally, community leaders and parents should be sufficiently informed to become a positive resource for the program.

In community service programs where schools or agencies send young people to community organizations that receive them as workers, it is essential that clear and definite areas of responsibilities be established and that collaboration and cooperation continue between the "sending" and "receiving" agencies.

While it is possible that only a few adults will be directly involved, it is most important that all pertinent staff in both the "sending" and "receiving" organizations be informed about all aspects of the project and that they thoroughly understand the work to be undertaken by the youth. Indeed, efforts should be made to try to win to the philosophy of experiential education not only the school principal or agency executives, but others whose support will be needed, including the building custodian and the staff supervising the students in the community. Often needless anxieties develop simply through lack of information; this can sabotage a program before it has had time to fully develop or start.

While adults serve more as a supportive presence than an active influence in most youth participation programs, it is they who must retain responsibility for the quality of the experience. All will not be serene. It is unreasonable to suppose that young people who have had little prior experience with responsibility will shoulder it with ease. Adults should understand that some frustrations and discouragements are inherent in all social decision-making. Yet, they should have faith in untested youthful capabilities, respond to limitless needs, and admit vulnerability. In addition, adult leaders must maintain that delicate balance between ambiguity and chaos. On the one hand, there is the temptation to take over—when students seem especially inept, the adult can issue a few quick orders and get the program on its way. The accomplishments may be impressive, but the young people will have been squelched again, denied even an apprenticeship in decision-making. The other extreme is to give no direction—permitting students' discussions to circle endlessly around decisions without ever grasping at one and translating it into action. Meanwhile, intentions disintegrate, self-confidence collapses, and frustration sets in. Adults must chart a course between these two equally disastrous extremes. The young people must sense that both their decisions will be respected and that great things are expected of them. If they suspect that their planning can be annulled by adult fiat, they are less likely to feel committed to their work. Nor will they feel responsible if the adult does not set firm standards that indicate his own sense of responsibility to the program.

By now the reader may be wondering where one ever finds

adults with the exemplary qualities needed to work with young people in youth participation projects. Special though they may be, they do exist in all communities, schools, churches, agencies, and other institutions. Recognizing the plight of many young people who are oversupplied with information but impoverished when it comes to the real-life skills and experiences necessary for successful adulthood, these individuals are waiting for the challenges and opportunities of the experiential learning method.

Redressing the imbalance in the lives of young people may seem an overwhelming task. Indeed, the magnitude of the challenge is exceeded only by the dangers of leaving adolescents unequipped to make decisions in a world where alternatives multiply at a dizzying rate. Experiential learning may prove to be the most important means for meeting this monumental challenge. The door this mode of learning opens is always outward onto a range of almost limitless possibilities. Determined teachers and administrators need only marshal the energy and imagination that lie latent in every American school and youth-serving agency—the energies and imagination that are helping preserve the forests of Maine and clean up the waters of Coos Bay.

Selected sources of further information

COUNT US IN, Mora and Alec Dickson, Dobson Books Ltd., 80 Kensington Church St., London, 1967. Many how-to suggestions for developing community service projects.

FLOWERS CAN EVEN BLOOM IN SCHOOLS, ed. by M. Perlstein, Westinghouse Learning Press, 770 Lucerne Way, Sunnyvale, Calif. Essays by educators who are both practitioners and theorists. They identify selected innovative programs and examine the psychological and educational principles that underlie them, with emphasis on the affective processes for both teachers and students in experiential learning, student autonomy, and other new options.

FORTY PROJECTS BY GROUPS OF KIDS, National Commission on Resources for Youth, 36 West 44th St., New York, 1973. One- to three-page descriptions of forty projects developed by young persons in cooperation with adults. Includes projects in legal services, day care and teaching, community arts, and community service.

HIGH SCHOOL STUDENT VOLUNTEERS, ACTION, Government Printing Office, Washington, D.C., 1973. Information about how to develop community service and volunteer programs.

RESOURCES FOR YOUTH, National Commission on Resources for Youth, 36 West 44th St., New York. A quarterly newsletter describing outstanding examples of youth participation projects. Readers may contact the Commission for write-ups from its files of more than 800 youth participation projects and may order films and videotapes about youth participation projects from their library of audio-visual materials.

SCHOOL AND COMMUNITY KITS, published bimonthly by the Community Service Volunteers, 237 Pentonville Rd., London. Also publishes pamphlets and other kits to guide adults and young people in developing community service projects.

SYNERGIST, published three times yearly by the National Student Volunteer Program ACTION, 806 Connecticut Ave., N.W., Washington, D.C. Articles about youth volunteer projects in the United States and abroad.

YOUTH INTO ADULTS, M. McCloskey and P. Kleinbard, National Commission on Resources for Youth, 36 West 44th St., New York, 1974. Ten case studies of youth participation programs. Describes the educational principles underlying each and offers practical suggestions for developing programs.

Addresses of current projects

BERKELEY YOUTH COUNCIL, Berkeley City Hall, Berkeley, Calif. 94704

BLACK SPECTRUM or HARLEM YOUTH SPEAKS, The New York Times, c/o Community Affairs Director, 229 West 43rd St., New York, N.Y. 10036

CHERRY CREEK SCHOOLS, 4700 South Yosemite St., Englewood, Colo. 80110

THE CITY ARTS WORKSHOP, 58 Ludlow St., New York, N.Y. 10002

CLINTON PROGRAM, Clinton Junior High School, 314 West 54th St., New York, N.Y. 10019

CONSUMER EDUCATION, Students Teaching Our Public (STOP), Patrick Henry High School, 6702 Wandermere Dr., San Diego, Calif. 92120

CORONA-EAST ELMHURST TRANSITION PRESS, Community Affairs Director, The New York Times, 229 West 43rd St., New York, N.Y. 10036

DUO, State Department of Education, Montpelier, Vt. 05602

EARTH, Campolindo High School, 300 Moraga Rd., Moraga, Calif. 94556

EDUCAGE, 33 Church St., White Plains, N.Y. 10602

ELEMENTARY INSTITUTE OF SCIENCE, 608 51st St., San Diego, Calif. 92114

ENFIELD SOCIAL STUDIES LABORATORY, Enfield High School, Enfield, Conn. 06030

FEAST, Jefferson High School, Portland, Oreg. 97207

THE FOURTH STREET I, c/o Brigade in Action, 136 Ave. C, New York, N.Y. 10009

FOXFIRE, Rabun Gap, Ga. 30568

FRIEND TO FRIEND PROGRAM, Jewish Social Service Agency, 6123 Montrose Rd., Rockville, Md. 20852

HIGH SCHOOL ARCHAELOGY PROJECT, Atlanta Public Schools, Instructional Services Center, 2930 Forrest Hill Dr., S.W., Atlanta, Ga. 30315

HOYEKIYA, Box 282, Pine Ridge, S.Dak. 57770

MALE STUDENTS AS TEACHER ASSISTANTS, Louisville Public Schools, 506 West Hill, Louisville, Ky. 40208

MANUAL HIGH SCHOOL, 1700 East 28th Ave., Denver, Colo. 80205

METRO, 537 South Dearborn St., Chicago, Ill. 60605

MUSEUM OF THE HUDSON HIGHLANDS, Cornwall-on-Hudson, N.Y. 12520

NATIONAL COMMISSION ON RESOURCES FOR YOUTH, 36 West 44th St., New York, N.Y. 10036

OKLAHOMANS FOR INDIAN OPPORTUNITY, 555 Constitution, Norman, Okla. 73069

ONTARIO-MONTCLAIR SCHOOL DISTRICT, 950 West D St., P.O. Box 313, Ontario, Calif. 91761

PEER COUNSELING PROGRAM, Dept. of Psychiatry, Stanford Medical Center, Stanford, Calif. 94304

PROJECT SELF, Vancouver Secondary Schools, Lord Bynd School, Vancouver, British Columbia, Canada

RAMAPO SCHOOL AND COMMUNITY SERVICE PROGRAM, Ramapo Central School District No. 2, 50-A South Main St., Spring Valley, N.Y. 10977

RENT-A-KID, Metro Commission on Crime, Atlanta, Ga. 30304

SCHOOL-COMMUNITY SERVICE, San Mateo Union High School District, 650 North Delaware St., San Mateo, Calif. 94401

SONOMA PROJECT, First Congregational Church, 1985 Louis Rd., Palo Alto, Calif. 94303

STUDENT AID TRAINING PROGRAM, O.H. Close School for Boys, Stockton, Calif. 95202

STUDENT BOARD OF EDUCATION, Santa Barbara High School District, 720 Santa Barbara St., Santa Barbara, Calif. 93101

STUDENT COALITION FOR RELEVANT SEX EDUCATION, c/o Planned Parenthood, 300 Park Ave. South, New York, N.Y. 10010

STUDENT-COMMUNITY INVOLVEMENT PROJECT, Center for Youth Development and Research, 301 Walter Library, Minneapolis, Minn. 54555

STUDENT CURRICULUM EXPERIENCE PROJECT, Petaluma Unified School District, 11 Fifth St., Petaluma, Calif. 94952

STUDENT TUTORIAL AND ASSISTANT TEACHER PROGRAM, Jefferson High School, 5210 North Kerby, Portland, Oreg. 97217

STUDENTS CONCERNED WITH PUBLIC HEALTH, c/o Ray Kauffman, 501 Oak St., Millersburg, Pa. 17061

TEACHERS AND WRITERS COLLABORATIVE, c/o P.S. 3, 490 Hudson St., New York, N.Y. 10014

TECHNICAL RECREATION CENTER, 910 Central Ave., North Wildwood, N.J. 08260

TUTORIAL COMMUNITY PROJECT, 12961 Van Nuys Blvd., Pacoima, Calif. 91331

UNWINDING ROOM, Maria Goretti High School, 10th and Moore Sts., Philadelphia, Pa. 19148

THE YOUNG FILMMAKERS, 6 Rivington St., New York, N.Y. 10002

YOUNG WORLD DEVELOPMENT PROGRAM, American Freedom from Hunger Foundation, 1717 H St., N.W., Washington, D.C. 20037

YOUTH ADVOCATES, 1301½ Pike St., Seattle, Wash. 98122

YOUTH AND THE FOREIGN BORN, International Institute of the East Bay, 297 Lee St., Oakland, Calif. 74610

YOUTH CITIZENSHIP FUND, INC., 2100 M St., N.W., Washington, D.C. 20037

YOUTH ELDERLY SERVICES (YES), Family Service of Greater Fall River, 101 Rock St., Fall River, Mass. 02720

YOUTH TO YOUTH ON DRUG ABUSE, San Francisco Unified School District, 135 Van Ness Ave., San Francisco, Calif. 94102

3 — 1303—00032-7016